ENGLISH EMBROIDERY

ENGLISH EMBROIDERY

Barbara Snook

Mills & Boon Ltd London

First published in Great Britain 1960 by B. T. Batsford Ltd.
This edition published 1974 by Mills and Boon Limited,
17-19 Foley Street, London W1A 1DR.

ISBN 0 263 05579 5

Printed photolitho in Great Britain
by Ebenezer Baylis & Son Limited
The Trinity Press, Worcester, and London

Contents

Acknowledgment

To Miss Iris Hills is offered my most sincere thanks for her suggestion that I should write an embroidery book, which in fact developed into two, this one and its predecessor *Learning to Embroider*. I am also indebted to Mr. H. M. Nixon, Deputy Keeper of the Department of Printed Books at the British Museum, and to Miss M. Pilkington, formerly Honorary Director of the Whitworth Art Gallery, Manchester, for their kindness in allowing me to examine at leisure a large collection of embroidered book bindings and a varied selection of English embroidery.

For detailed information on Opus Anglicanum I have drawn extensively on Mrs. A. H. Christie's authoritative book, *English Mediaeval Embroidery*, which is not readily available to many people.

The Victoria and Albert Museum has the finest collection in the world of European embroidery and publishes excellently illustrated booklets; it is inevitable that many references should be made to specimens in the Museum's possession, but in addition to these more familiar examples an effort has been made to gather together a series of drawings of work not so easily accessible.

I am most grateful to my friends for their helpful comments, especially to Miss Lefa Fry for her thorough scrutiny and correction of the manuscript, and to Messrs. B. T. Batsford Ltd. for their constant help and the care they took in the publication of the first edition. I and the present publishers are also grateful to them for allowing this book to appear under another imprint.

For permission to quote extracts from the following books, I would like to thank:

Professor D. Talbot Rice, *English Art 871–1100*, published by the Oxford University Press; Professor G. M. Trevelyan, *History of England*, Longman Group Limited; G. Wingfield Digby, *The Bayeux Tapestry* (General Editor, Sir Frank Stenton), Phaidon Press Limited.

Introduction

The preface to a 17th-century pattern book declares that "maids" like "Squirrell skip from tree to tree", learning a little of many kinds of stitchery until proficient in all. Certainly their predecessors had during 700 years so practised the art of embroidery that it had become an established part of our heritage. Today we profit from the accumulated knowledge of a further 300 years.

The development of this tradition is as fascinating as that of all other crafts and at various times in our history the embroiderer has been held in as high repute as the metal-worker, stonemason, wood-carver and illuminator; indeed from 1250–1350 English pre-eminence in embroidery was acknowledged throughout Europe.

Much of a country's history can be learned from its crafts. Styles and methods change according to contemporary needs and taste and sometimes fashions sweep through many different crafts at once as in the 18th century the cult for things Chinese affected table-silver, bedsteads, and the appurtenances of the tea table.

Comparatively few examples of early embroidery remain in existence so that much of our knowledge comes secondhand from written records such as wills and inventories, monumental brasses and manuscripts. Excellent work is distributed among the world's museums and private collections but we know that far more has been lost than has been saved, because the basic material has perished, destroyed by damp, dirt, fire and moth, and by the depredations of man who is not always appreciative of beauty, and besides cutting things up to put them to another use, has not hesitated to steal jewels or melt down gold thread in time of need.

Only when we consider that there is in existence Coptic (Egyptian Christian) work of the 3rd and 4th century A.D. and Chinese silk embroidery of the Tang dynasty, A.D. 618–906, from the Cave of the Thousand Buddhas, in Mongolia, so fine that it can only have been the result of many centuries of experience, do we realise that in this craft our own development has been comparatively late, for the story of English embroidery does not begin until the early 10th century.

Yet this earliest extant example, the Durham stole, is of such astonishing skill that we can but assume that here too is the result of long-established tradition, no other example of which remains to us.

1   *Detail from Abigail Pett's bed hangings. Early 17th century*

In tracing the growth of the craft from this point we may speak of the 16th, 17th or 18th centuries, of the Tudor or Stuart periods or of Queen Anne or Victorian styles, yet these are all fluid terms, made for our convenience, and however we may try to put history into neat compartments, we shall fail because of the steady growth of ideas which cannot be bound by precise dates. Most of all it is important to grasp the continuity of ideas, to understand their growth and to appreciate the beautiful, albeit sometimes curious, work that has come down to us.

Men and women of earlier generations cannot have been indifferent to the embroidery which enhanced the pageantry of church, battlefield and tournament. They must have enjoyed wearing their distinctive clothes and can hardly have failed to be impressed with their own magnificence: we today are in our turn excited by state ceremonial, forgetful that such splendour was once much more commonplace. They must also have enjoyed less ostentatious objects handled every day—embroidered book covers, cushions, quilts, whether made for them by members of their households or with their own fingers expressing their own individuality. Need we quite so airily dismiss our lack of patience by saying that there is no place in the modern world for fine embroidery, knowing only too well the difference even one piece of good craftsmanship, no matter what the craft, can make to our sense of well-being in a cherished home?

If some of these exquisite things have come to us by accident others certainly have been handed down deliberately, for their owners were well aware of the quality of their work, though none can possibly have dreamt that hundreds of years into the future their caps, coifs, tiny bags and tent stitch covered chairs would become museum treasures of such extremely great value.

Mediaeval Embroidery

ANGLO-SAXON

If Anglo-Saxon England seems a remote period in our history, this may be because so little remains of people's handiwork, yet the comparatively few treasures which have been found show that in several crafts a degree of perfection was reached of which we may well be envious. A culture is often judged by its architecture and because the Anglo-Saxons built in wood, a perishable material, there has, until recently, been a tendency to overlook their other achievements. These wooden homes, even of the nobility, cannot have been cosy places in which to live, and attempts must have been made to exclude draughts by means of curtains made of narrow widths of home-spun woollen fabric sewn together probably with some form of stitchery, as in an 8th-century fragment in the Whitworth Art Gallery, Manchester (2). From this desire to make the home warm, then attractive, came the inspiration to decorate these woven strips with a record of valiant deeds and to work pictures of ancient legends. Such hangings must have been very treasured possessions, and they would have been taken by their owners wherever they moved.

2 *8th-century seam on a fragment.*
(*Whitworth Art Gallery, Manchester*)

Written records show that from the 9th century in Europe embroidery was taught in royal households and monasteries where robes for court and church festivals and the banners, which were to be carried in battle, were made. The gold and silk needed came, as it did for many years, from Cyprus and Venice; needles at this time were probably of bone, delicately fashioned. Two examples of embroidery from this early date have survived—the stole and maniple of St. Cuthbert, now at Durham, which were probably made in Winchester as early as A.D. 905–10, during the time when it was the capital and a great art centre (3). The workmanship is remarkable for several reasons—silk stitchery so closely covers the

ground fabric that it is almost impossible to decide whether it is of linen (Mrs. A. H. Christie) or silk (Talbot Rice); it is the only surviving example of the use of pure gold, so fine that sixteen threads laid side by side cover only $\frac{1}{8}''$; to give contrast, within the outline of the haloes, it is laid to a diaper pattern, no mean technical feat.[1]

[1] "St. Cuthbert's stole and maniple, and a few smaller pieces. Stole . . . fragments $2\frac{3}{8}''$ wide and now 6' long. Maniple . . . fragments $2\frac{3}{8}''$ wide and now 2' $8\frac{1}{4}''$ long. Both thickly embroidered with saints and prophets, with Christian symbols and a border of acanthus scrolls and pairs of confronted animals.

"*On the stole* are 13 saints and prophets on conventionalised clouds; names in large letters on either side of the figures.

"*On the maniple* are St. Sixtus, St. Gregory and the deacons Lawrence and Peter.

"It shows the Byzantine influence on the Anglo-Saxon world. The lettering has a decorative value beyond indicating the name." (*English Art*, 871–1100. Talbot Rice. O.U.P., 1952.)

It is interesting to read, too, Professor Talbot Rice's reasons for the precise dating of this work.

3   *St. Cuthbert's maniple; 10th century (Durham Cathedral). Linen embroidered with coloured silks in split stitch, stem stitch and couched work in gold thread and red silk*

NORMAN CONQUEST

A gap of over 150 years separates the Durham stole and the next extant work, the Bayeux tapestry, one of the most famous embroideries in the world(4). Much has been written about it and recently an exhaustive study, excellently illustrated, has been published. A tapestry is a woven hanging made on a loom, therefore the Bayeux tapestry, which is embroidered, is not technically a tapestry at all, though that is its usual name. Made to hang on the walls of the church of Bishop Odo of Bayeux, it is on a long strip of linen, 230' $10\frac{1}{4}'' \times 19\frac{3}{4}''$, worked in shades of wool, terra cotta, blue-green, buff, blue, darker green, yellow, and very dark blue; eight recognisable colours, with variations in dye and fading. Couching, laid-work and outline stitch are used. The areas of laid-work have detail upon them in lines of couching and everything is outlined which helps to bind the colours together.

Its survival may be due to two factors; linen is tough and enduring and the wool embroidered upon it could not be reclaimed for any other use. Other pictorial work of the period, using gold, silver thread and jewels, has been lost because the valuable materials were pillaged.

For many years a doubt existed as to whether it was made in

4   *The Bayeux Tapestry. "Some of the English are isolated upon a hillock and attacked"*

France or England, a problem now resolved; though the exact date is uncertain, it was worked in England, perhaps at Canterbury, very soon after the Conquest. The detailed story and similarities in the style of drawing in 11th-century English manuscripts, for instance the interlacing tree branches, have led to this conclusion. Professor Talbot Rice calls it a panorama showing

> the events of Harold's life preceding the conquest as well as the story of the actual conquest itself and the progress of the Normans up to the death of Harold at Hastings. The story is told in a completely dispassionate, historical manner, favouring neither one side nor the other, yet it is amazingly vivid. The tapestry is in fact one of the most enchanting pieces of narrative art in existence.

G. W. Digby tells us that

> it was intended to be hung in public, presumably in the nave of Bayeux Cathedral, where in fact it is known to have been yearly hung for so many centuries. It was designed to tell a story to a largely illiterate public; it is like a strip cartoon, racy, emphatic, colourful, with a good deal of blood and thunder and some ribaldry. But it is also very exact in detail, full of contemporary life, and it shows the artist's imagination which seizes on essentials and has the power of transmitting them over the centuries. [1]

It is indeed a fascinating piece of work; the story is vigorously told and not entirely lacking in humour. Well-placed lettering explains certain situations and there are country incidents, bird-scaring and hunting, and fables, such as the Raven and Fox, in the margins, as well as an overflow of the main theme. The few colours are used without relation to fact, so that a horse may have one fore-leg green with a red hoof while the other is yellow with a green hoof. Forests and buildings are suggested with great economy; there is no perspective, nor are people and objects drawn to scale, but the artists had little to learn about dramatic gesture and in this respect their work has never been surpassed.

Yet for all its historical and perhaps entertainment value, it should be remembered that as with all mediaeval art its purpose was religious, it was designed for a church and "its aim was to show the fulfilment of God's judgement on the violated oath sworn by Harold at Bayeux". [2]

[1] *The Bayeux Tapestry*, Phaidon Press.   [2] Professor Lethaby.

ECCLESIASTICAL

The Bayeux Tapestry appears as a primitive piece of drawing coming between the Durham stole, which reflects Byzantine culture, and the ecclesiastical embroideries of the 13th century, which remain our greatest achievement in design and technique. During these 300 years the monasteries had fostered learning and the arts.

Only a few fragments of 12th-century embroidery exist now. When the tomb of Bishop William de Blois, in Worcester Cathedral was opened, a much disintegrated stole and maniple and other pieces of fabric were found. These belong to the first half of the 12th century and are technically rather clumsy. Figures are worked on a brownish red silk ground in gold and silk. The hair is in gold underside couching and the faces, hands and feet are roughly worked in underside couching in silk(5). Detail is shown with lines of darker silk. The fabric is edged with a line of fine gold feather stitch.

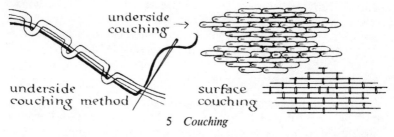

5   *Couching*

Fortunately of the later period much more evidence is available. The mid 13th to mid 14th century is the period of highest achievement in the history of embroidery. From 1250–1350 ecclesiastical embroidery was of an exceptionally high standard of design and little short of miraculous in technique. Small wonder that it found favour abroad and that copes and chasubles sent as gifts provoked orders for more of the work which is still known today by the name it then acquired—Opus Anglicanum—and known, too, to refer to embroidery and no other craft. In the choice of fabric, thread and stitches, European and English embroidery had, at this time, much in common and the technical standard was everywhere high. The use of gold was universal, and as much was used in the Byzantine style vestments made for the Greek Orthodox church as for the Roman Catholic church. Inevitably many vestments reached Rome from all over Europe, therefore English work must have been of outstanding quality to evoke favourable Papal comment, and subsequent orders would have further stimulated designers and embroiderers.

There are several characteristics which distinguished Opus Anglicanum from other contemporary work in addition to its marked superiority in the technique of handling gold thread and silk. Each country has its own saints and these were included with others of general significance. It would be surprising indeed to find St. Edmund of Bury on any other than an English vestment. Heraldry too provides a means of identification.[1] Coats of arms may not always have played as prominent a part as they do in the design of the Syon cope, but frequently occurred, as in the design of an early 14th-century stole and maniple in the Victoria and Albert Museum, entirely composed of coats of arms worked in plaited stitch. In the general layout of the design, barbed quatrefoils(10) are favoured rather than the simple quatrefoils used in European work; arcading is foliated and crockets are more developed, all small points in themselves yet contributing to the final richness of design. Figure drawing is dramatic in pose, facial expression and gesture, the effect intensified by large heads, eyes, hands and feet—all too large for there to be any idealisation of the characters(6, 11). The skin is always in split stitch, a method also

used in Germany, but here worked spirally from a deep depression in the centre, a method perhaps devised to catch the play of light upon silk or merely as an expedient to break up an otherwise plain surface. Detail is added with a clear dark outline as if skilfully drawn with a pen.

Yet another distinguishing feature, and one which can be traced henceforward in English embroidery, is the predilection for wild life, particularly birds and animals about which information could

6 *Detail from panel of about 1300, "Christ charging the Apostles". (British Museum)*

[1] Heraldry, see Bibliography.

7 *Angel swinging a censer from the Anagni cope, late 13th century; design between roundels. Worked in gold and silver underside couching with more silver than usual. The censer is silver on a gilt chain; wings and drapery are in blue and madder pink silk in split stitch. The whole cope has very dramatically told incidents from the lives of Christ and the Virgin*

be gleaned from Bestiaries and sketch books such as that now in the Library of Magdalene College, Cambridge, a proven source of inspiration. There are as yet very few recognisable plants, other than daisy, columbine, rose, lily and oak: the vine, a long-established Christian symbol, is more naturalistically treated than in European work. Lettering, when used to explain a subject or a character otherwise unidentifiable through lack of attributes, is in the Lombardic style(8); abbreviations similar to those in manuscripts, such as $\overline{DNI}$ for domini, are found.

All Opus Anglicanum was worked in a frame. The mediaeval love of large areas of gold, seen in other crafts, particularly in manuscripts of the East Anglian school and in the panel painting of Richard II in the National Gallery, made this a necessity; moreover, laid gold cannot be worked in the hand.

Three materials were used for a ground. Fine linen, mounted above a coarser linen lining, was generally covered completely with laid gold and silk stitchery. Velvet, with a sheen which enhances

EPIPHANIA   8 *Lombardic lettering from a cope at Vich, near Barcelona; about 1325*

9 (1) *Motif in underside couching based on the design between roundels in the Ascoli Piceno cope 1275. Trilobed foliage is typical of late 12th to early 13th century ornament. Interlacing and the scroll can be traced through the history of embroidery* (2) *Pattern on the amice apparel, one of the vestments of St. Thomas of Canterbury at Sens Cathedral. Second half of the 12th century*

the lustre of gold, was backed with linen and had a fine linen laid over it, upon which the design was traced and which facilitated the passage of the needle through the pile; exposed parts of this upper layer were cut away afterwards, which cannot have been easy to do, but no trace shows unless the work is worn. Silk, which is also lined with linen, has, as a background fabric, the added advantage that gold can be used freely within the design, rather than on the background itself.

Embroidery was always in gold and silk. With the exception of the 10th-century Durham stole, in which pure gold was used, the metal thread is silver gilt, that is a fine strip of silver, covered with gold, wound over a silk core. It was underside couched with linen thread which also was used to pad raised gold.

Underside couching is a method which forms a very close union between fabric and thread producing so pliable a material that vestments upon which it was worked always hung well.

Floss silk, which could be stranded, was almost the only kind available. The representation of flesh was treated very delicately indeed and by comparison the silk was used more heavily for drapery. There were few stitches apart from underside couching and split stitch. Satin stitch and French knots were very rare; stem, overcast, cross, tent and plaited stitch appeared occasionally and a little surface couching and laid work, tied down with a trellis pattern, is found on the throne in the "Adoration of the Magi" panel in the Metropolitan Museum (New York) chasuble; a limited choice of stitches which is not without significance (12).

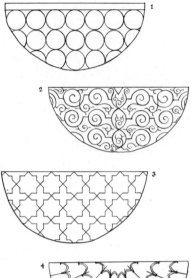

10   (1) *Ascoli Piceno, Anagni. Late 13th century*
(2) *Salzburg and Jesse (V. & A.) Late 12th–early 13th century*
(3) *Madrid, Syon, Vatican, Steeple Ashton, St. Bertrand-de-Comminges. Mid 13th–early 14th century*
(4) *Butler-Bowden, Vich, Bologna, Toledo, Pienza, and the cope of St. Sylvester. Early 14th century*

Mediaeval church ritual demanded a magnificent display for the glory of God and instruction of illiterate man. How much the congregation ever learned from the vestments is a moot point, for its view of them was a distant one; however, copes, chasubles, dalmatics, amices, stoles, maniples, mitres, buskins and sandals were lavishly decorated, as were altar frontals and dossals and fair linen cloths.

Of all these the cope had the largest field for design, and over so large an area a basic framework was needed to unite the diverse parts; this framework was in itself beautiful, and shows some continuity of development. A "Jesse" cope of the late 12th century–early 13th century, once in Salzburg, and another, incomplete, in the Victoria and Albert Museum have a scrolling design spreading from the central tree which arises from the recumbent figure of Jesse (10, 2). Geometric arrangements of circles or quatrefoils are used from the mid 13th to the early 14th century. Copes at Ascoli Piceno made in 1275 and given to the Pope in 1288, and at Anagni Cathedral, made in the late 13th century are examples of the circular style (10, 1); the cope of St. Bertrand-de-Comminges has a similar basis (10, 3); the Syon and Madrid copes and one in the Vatican, are based on the barbed quatrefoil, as is that of Steeple Ashton which is also foliated (10, 3). In the last and most mature phase of Opus Anglicanum, *c.* 1330, the design is arcaded; copes at

Pienza, Toledo, Bologna, Vich (near Barcelona), the cope of St. Sylvester, once in the Basilica of St. John Lateran, Rome, and now in the Vatican Museum, and the Butler-Bowden cope (V. & A.), are all examples of this style (10, ₄).

All are of outstanding beauty. The cope in the Cathedral at St. Bertrand-de-Comminges shows more than any other, in the small linking compartments of the design, delight in birds and animals, here at their most numerous; there are 34 birds and 66 beasts, no two being alike and all recognisable species, exquisitely drawn.

The Steeple Ashton fragment is on a pale fawn twill silk ground, lined with linen. It is worked almost entirely in gold underside couching, with silk split stitch for faces, hands and feet, and silver for symbols and some details. Meandering boughs of oak and ivy linked by human-headed masks, form the barbed quatrefoils which contain scenes from the life of Christ and the Virgin, showing action in the figures and a strong sense of narrative. Vigorously drawn heraldic lions fill the spaces between.[1]

It should not be difficult to study the Syon cope carefully because pictures of it are reproduced in so many books and encyclopedias. Such study is worth while in spite of the fact that though it has many features typical of Opus Anglicanum it is not the best work of the time. The geometric design is based on interlaced barbed quatrefoils outlined in gold; their ground is covered in red silk now faded to a soft pink and the intervening spaces are in green. This is the only example with a silk stitchery ground, with the use of a different colour within and without the quatrefoil; possibly the silk

[1] Copes embroidered with silk against a gold thread background, therefore upon a two-fold linen base:
Ascoli Piceno, which has a very small hood
Anagni
Salzburg
Madrid
Toledo
Bologna
Pienza
St. Bertrand-de-Comminges
The cope of St. Sylvester. This is one of the finest examples from every point of view; it retains its very tiny original hood; some tent stitch is used. Height 5' 2½", width 11½', orphrey 9" wide, hood 7" high × 8" wide, morse 6" × 3½"
Copes upon a silk ground, linen lined, worked with silk and gold thread:
Vatican
Jesse (V. & A.)
Copes upon a velvet ground, worked in silk and gold thread:
Vich
Butler-Bowden

was a later addition. It is worked in underside couching to give a chevron pattern on the surface. The quatrefoils contain scenes from the life of Christ and the Virgin, and figures of St. Michael and the Apostles. Six-winged seraphim, some with peacock feather or eyed wings, a characteristic of Opus Anglicanum, are in each of the green spaces. The delicately drawn figures and drapery are worked entirely in fine split stitch. There is a narrow band of heraldry around the semicircular edge of the cope and the orphrey is composed of fourteen heraldic shields in the form of lozenges and roundels. The morse also carries an emblem. All the heraldic work, which is in cross stitch, long-armed cross stitch and couched work, may have been added later.

The early 14th-century Butler-Bowden cope, also in the Victoria and Albert Museum, is arcaded upon a red velvet ground. It appears to be one of a series from a workshop, an occurrence probably much more common than we usually imagine. There is a similar cope at Vich. A chasuble in the Metropolitan Museum, New York (12), is of so much greater vigour, in gesture and in the lively tilt of angel's wing feathers as to make even the Butler-Bowden cope appear inanimate. The illustration is taken from the New York chasuble and the parallel scene in the cope should be

(*Continued on page 24*)

11   (1) *Detail from a late 13th-century orphrey (Musée historique des tissus, Lyon), showing King David seated on a cushioned throne. He wears a blue fur-lined mantle over a red-fawn vest; all drapery is in split stitch; a jewelled crown rests upon hair striped Indian red and shaded green, and his beard is green. Cheeks are worked in spirals with a deep depression in the centre. He is playing, with an over-large hand characteristic of Opus Anglicanum, a yellow harp. The throne is laid silk, tied with surface couched trellis stitch outlined with gold. Throughout the orphrey haloes and crowns are of gold. The treatment of the vine is of particular interest and is unique in the amount of tent stitch which on all the leaves is minutely worked over a single thread of linen, in yellowish gold silk; each grape is padded laid silk, outlined in gold. The stem is in three shades of green. The entire background is in gold underside couching*
(2A) *Geometric construction of the St. Bertrand-de-Comminges cope to show the position of birds and animals*
(2B) *Foliated design on the circles*
(3) *Part of a foliated barbed quatrefoil on the Steeple Ashton cope*
(4) *Detail from a fragment of the orphrey belonging to the Steeple Ashton cope. It is upon a pale fawn twill silk ground. The background is covered entirely with underside couching and all silk stitchery is in split stitch*
(5) *Peacock feathers*

1

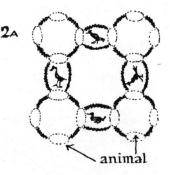

2A

animal

2B

3

4

5

compared with it(12). There are two slight differences in detail;
where the cope has three crockets on each arch and four twists in
the foliated arcading, the chasuble has four crockets and three
twists. Technique in both is supremely good. In addition to the

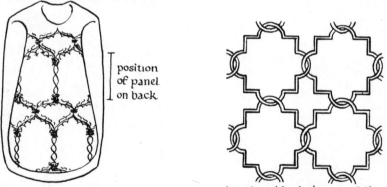

12   *The "Adoration of the Magi" from the back of the chasuble in the Metro-*
politan Museum, New York. A stole and maniple were also made from fragments
cut from the chasuble. This shows a typical arcaded setting with crockets above
and cusps below each arch

richness of so much gold on velvet, pearls, most of which have long since vanished, were used in quantity; according to Mrs. Christie: "The parts once enriched with pearls now show a surface of lightly stitched white silk, the usual underlay for such ornament. It is seen on stars, crowns, and other accessories of the scenes and figures, also on the lion's masks and acorns of the arcading."

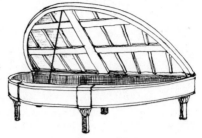

13   *Salisbury Cathedral cope chest*

Vestments such as these had to be carefully stored. Both York Minster and Salisbury Cathedral possess mediaeval cope chests; that of York is in two parts necessitating a fold down the centre of the cope, the cause of frequent damage, for it was there that the embroidery wore thin most quickly and either had to be repaired or the whole garment remodelled; that of Salisbury (13) is one large semicircle.

Fewer chasubles than copes have been preserved because the early bell-shaped style ceased to be used. One very fine example of the old shape, dated about 1300, is now in Vienna (14). It is unusual in that there is only one pictorial subject, the Crucifixion, on each side, showing successive stages of the tragedy with all the usual

14   *Bell-shaped Vienna chasuble, about 1300, circumference 16' 8", showing cuts for armholes and approximate position of the Crucifixion scene*

vigour in pose and facial expression, with large eyes, black outlines and spiral stitchery, characteristic of Opus Anglicanum. The embroidery fortunately was unharmed when at some later date the garment was mutilated by large cuts for armholes. A front view of the wild rose is so closely associated in our minds with the Tudor period that it is a surprise to find it used here in a background of barbed quatrefoils, taking pride of place while four delicately drawn vine leaves are relegated to the smaller intervening spaces. The purple twill silk ground is embroidered in gold and silver thread, mainly in underside couching, and in silks, several shades of brown, buff, yellow, amber, a pink which may once have been red, myrtle and yellow-green, white and black. The roses have white petals worked spirally in split stitch; they are outlined with gold which is also used in the centre. The vine leaves too have a gold outline, two are yellow with green veins and two are in shades of pink.

Smaller articles of apparel were treated with no less interest. The shape of the mitre has changed from a simple triangle to the shape we know today, but does not appear to have done so progressively because two of the early 13th century are triangular whereas that reputed to have belonged to St. Thomas of Canterbury, of the second half of the 12th century, is similar to those now in use. St. Thomas' mitre is worked in silver gilt on a diapered silk cloth (15). It is a vertical band and border of rose-pink silk upon which needle perforations still show, an indication that it was once embroidered. The remaining space is decorated with scrolls and roundels which have now lost their ornament, probably of jewels. The outline of circles, scrolls and leaves is of gold thread worked in underside couching. Originally the lappets were alike: a little feather stitch can be found on

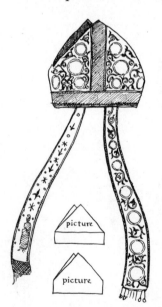

15   *St. Thomas of Canterbury's mitre*

them and on the mitre. As in the Durham stole, the foliage is not naturalistic.

Buskins were long embroidered stockings. The only complete English pair was found in a tomb in Canterbury. These, of the early 13th century, are very faded but may have been green. They are ornamented with a net diaper of gold thread, each compartment containing a small star or cross device, or an eagle. Even the feet, which would have been hidden by sandals, are powdered with six rayed stars and crosses and spots of gold (16).

There are fragmentary buskins in the British Museum and the Victoria and Albert Museum worked in gold and a dark brown silk outline on purplish-brown twill silk which show enough of a scrolling Tree of Jesse to suggest the whole design. Other fragments are in Worcester Cathedral and at Sens.

Each of the sandals, also found at Canterbury, is made of a single piece of silk, probably green, lined with amber tinted damask silk, and has a red silk sole. They are richly decorated with gold and silver in underside couching and with gems. The design includes the lion, dragon and eagle and a cross device; carbuncles and fleurs-de-lis enriched a border along the top edge. It is interesting that so much attention was given to garments almost entirely hidden from view (16).

16   *Buskin and sandal found at Canterbury*

17   (1) *Early 13th-century fragment from Southwark Cathedral of a knight on horseback. Worked in gold, silver and coloured silks on rose-tinted twill silk, over coarse canvas. There are six gold threads to $\frac{1}{16}$". Except for some stem stitch outlining, underside couching is used. The horse is in gold and has a buff eye outlined in stem stitch. The harness is silver, and a silver band with tassels secures the trapping which is underside couched with ultramarine silk. The bridle is outlined. The knight wears a silver helmet with gold bands. His eye and cheek are in buff silk couching. On the skirt of his gold coat of mail a few short silver stitches are scattered across the gold. His legs are in gold with a silver stirrup and spur. The shield is blazoned, gules, a chief indented or—incorporating the red silk of the ground fabric; $3\frac{3}{4}" \times 4\frac{1}{2}"$*

(2) *Lion from an early 13th-century cope in Herzog-Anton Ulrich Museum, Brunswick. The cope is powdered with stars, lions and displayed eagles, in gold upon rose-tinted silk*

(3) *A fragment mounted on a green velvet of a knight on horseback, worked in split stitch and raised gold and silver thread and silk on linen; known as the Stonyhurst knight; about $8\frac{1}{2}"$ high*

Yet this is but typical of the mediaeval craftsman's attitude towards his work, and no more incongruous than the stone-mason's detail placed high in the clerestory or dark in the crypt, the woodcarver's misericorde or top of a rood screen, invisible to human eye. The aim was perfection, with honest pride in attainment, in fine work done for the greater glory of God.

A few examples of the burse or corporal case[1] have come down to us. One owned by Oscott College, Birmingham, made about 1300, is worked with gold and silver thread and coloured silks on linen. In the figures of the Apostles St. Peter and St. Paul the split stitch is fine but the rest of the work is rather coarse.

Not all Opus Anglicanum is as perfect as the panel in the British Museum, which must be one of the finest extant. Worked about 1300, it depicts Christ charging the Apostles, and the Betrayal. The split stitch on robes and skin is so small as to be almost invisible. A fine dark outline is used for drawing in the features, fingers and toes. The angels have peacock feather wings and the design is arcaded. In two small panels—in the Victoria and Albert Museum —of St. Margaret and St. Catherine, and the Annunciation, which are embroidered in coloured silks in split stitch and underside couching in gold and silver thread, although the stitchery appears to have been worked directly upon the velvet for the pile shows through in worn places, there is an underlayer of fine yellow fabric which has been cut away. A velvet band (V. & A.) shows

[1] Corporal case—a thin stiff case about 8" square, laid on the chalice during Mass.

scenes from the life of Christ and the Virgin, a subject which, with
the Tree of Jesse, the mediaeval craftsman found full of dramatic
possibilities. The purpose of the large "Christ Enthroned" panel,
another of the Museum's treasures, is unknown. It is 3' 3½" high
×1' 4½" wide. In an arcaded setting, Christ, 2' 3", robed in a gold
mantle worn over a fawn silk tunic, both bordered with lions,
eagles and dragons, is seated on a cushioned throne. The nimbus
is richly decorated with large jewels upon a gold ground, and its
cross is studded with seed pearls. A background of blue twill silk,
linen lined, is powdered with gold lions rampant. Near the top of
the panel, in Lombardic script, is the name of the donor IOHANNIS
DE THANET and above are two small scenes of the Annunciation.
Gold and silver thread is worked in underside couching and all silk
is in split stitch.

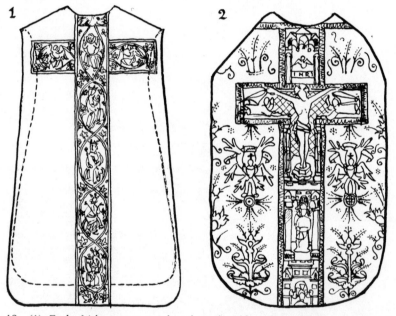

18   (1) *Early 14th-century purple velvet chasuble with orphreys embroidered
with gilt thread and coloured silks in split stitch and couched work; background of diapered gold; size 4' × 2' 5"; the back is illustrated, and the
front indicated by a dotted line*
(2) *Early 16th-century dark blue velvet chasuble with orphreys and ornament embroidered on linen with gilt thread and coloured silks, in split and
brick stitch and laid and couched work; 4' 2" × 3' 5"*

(1) *Amice*
(1A) *Apparel of the amice*
(1B) *Apparel of the dalmatic*
(2) *Alb*
(3) *Girdle*
(4) *Maniple*
(5) *Stole*
(6) *Chasuble; outer vestment of the celebrant at the Eucharist*
(6A) *Orphrey*
(7) *Biretta*
(8) *Dalmatic for Deacons Tunicle for Sub-Deacons*

19   *Vestments worn during the celebration of Mass*

The mediaeval flair for narrative can be seen in the 14th-century North German or French patchwork of red and blue cloth worked in hemmed appliqué, telling the story of the fight of a knight with a dragon, and in the English early 14th-century velvet band, worked in gold, silver and coloured silks showing the Annunciation, Visitation, Nativity, Angel appearing to the Shepherds and the Journey of the Magi. The fragment belonging to Stonyhurst College of a knight with sword upraised, seated upon a charging horse (17, 3) is as tantalising as that in Southwark Cathedral (17, 1), for the rest of these long vanished designs must have been treated with equal vigour.

The name Opus Anglicanum was not used after 1349. This was the year when the Black Death ravaged Europe. Craftsmen who survived this pestilence handed on their knowledge to the succeeding generation, but not necessarily the best workers lived to do so. A new term came into use, *façon d'Angleterre,* to describe the

20   *Angels* (1) *from the Syon cope, mid 13th–early 14th century, and* (2) *from an early 16th-century chasuble showing the difference in detail.*
(1) *all long feathers, drapery and halo are in gold underside couching: all short feathers, flesh and hair are in silk split stitch; everything has a dark outline.* x–y 10″
(2) *gold thread and coloured silks in split and brick stitch, laid and couched work are on linen applied to velvet.* x–y 8″

coarser style and less detailed drawing. Split stitch was still used but not in the distinguishing method for skin. It was accompanied by laid-work, couching, brick stitch, satin stitch and long and short stitch. Underside couching disappeared after the end of the 14th century. Even so, embroidery of the late 14th century sometimes achieved great richness; English and Continental pieces must have looked handsome and impressive in the religious ceremonies for which they were intended. Our appreciation of them suffers from inevitable comparison with the very unusual qualities of earlier work (18, 20). During the 15th century handsome brocades and velvets, fabrics so lovely in themselves that there could be no desire to cover them completely with embroidery, were imported from Venice. Motifs, worked on linen, were applied, scattered over the surface. On chasubles the orphrey alone was a continuously designed band. Of this period more chasubles than copes remain. These, though lacking in fine stitchery, have a certain individuality which is shown too in the 15th-century Chipping Campden altar frontal of white silk damask powdered with nondescript conventional devices. In this, a central figure of the Virgin, within a gold aureole, is

Lady's quilted dress in yellow satin with muslin apron. Early 18th century. Victoria and Albert Museum, Crown Copyright

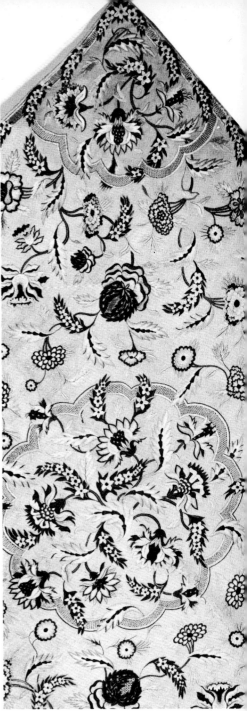

Part of an early 18th century coverlet which has matching pillows. Linen, quilted with yellow silk back stitch, and embroidered with red and yellow silks. Victoria and Albert Museum, Crown Copyright

Early 18th century hanging. Cotton twill embroidered with worsted threads in five colours. Stitches: long and short, stem, chain, flat, bullion and French knots, Cretan, detached chain, laid fillings and basket. Courtesy of The Embroiderers' Guild

Part of a hanging, about 1730-40. Knotted linen threads sewn on linen. Courtesy of the Chichester Estate and the City Museum and Art Gallery, Birmingham

supported on either side by two kneeling angels: the total effect is rather spiky and detail is coarse.

The Black Death, which marked an abrupt change in the style of many crafts, had a most serious effect upon embroidery. Over 150 years were to pass before a very high standard was again reached; in fact never again did such inspired design coincide with such perfection of technique in ecclesiastical work.

SECULAR AND DOMESTIC

The beauty of the mediaeval world is recorded for us in colour in Froissart's *Chronicles*, in *Les Très Riches Heures* of the Duc de Berri, 1416, in the Luttrell Psalter and other manuscripts, in a few early Flemish paintings, and in more sedate form, in brasses and effigies. Together these give a remarkably clear picture of the costume worn from about 1375–1500, so that, with written records, such as wardrobe accounts, issue rolls of the Exchequer, wills and inventories, we know something of the part played by embroidery not only in the decoration of clothes that have long since ceased to exist, but its growing use in the home and secular life of the country.

The arts of jousting and war were made more decorative by the Crusader's contact with the Middle East. The science of heraldry arose from the simple expedient devised to distinguish friend from foe upon the battle-field. Embroiderers were called upon to work blazons upon pennons and banners, jupons and caparisons. "King

21 *Jupon with arms of William de Fortibus, Earl of Albemarle, d. 1260, and his wife, Isabella de Redvers. Lion of blue linen, couched with red thread on to unbleached linen. All fine lines are in white thread. Teeth, white; eye, red. Cross of blue linen oversewn on to ground fabric; white linen is applied to the blue and sewn with blue couching. Height of fragment about 9"*

John ordered Reginald de Cornhill to furnish him with five banners with his arms embroidered on them, in 1215" (Jourdain). Many of these may have been painted but many more were worked in appliqué as can be seen in the Albemarle fragment now in the British Museum(21) which is of blue and white linen couched down with silk and has a little detail in outline stitch. One other very valuable example remains in this country—the jupon of the Black Prince. This quilted garment, made to be worn over armour, until recently hung above his tomb in Canterbury Cathedral. It shows the royal arms embroidered in gold thread and applied to the cloth, arranged quarterly, leopards upon a red velvet ground and fleurs-de-lis upon blue velvet.[1]

Yet another heraldic example is to be found in the Musée de Cluny, Paris(22). It may originally have been a horse-trapping but has been reshaped as a chasuble. It is of extremely fine deep pile red velvet, probably Persian. With three lions guardant in pale passant towards the sinister, as in seals of Edward I, II and III, it may have belonged to John of Eltham, second son of Edward II, or may even have been the coronation robe of Edward III. The lions are in gold, laid to represent hair and curling mane; the claws are raised, worked over blue silk; eyes are black and white, outlined in red and are covered with disks of crystal, under padded raised eyebrows; tongues are of red silk. The ground is closely covered with foliated scrolls and small figures of men and women worked in coloured silks, outlined with gold. It is a glorious piece of work full of the vigour that accompanies the best heraldic drawing.

[1] A reconstruction of the Jupon now hangs above the tomb in Canterbury Cathedral and gives a convincing idea of its original appearance.

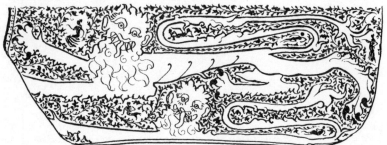

22   *Diagram showing half the back of a chasuble made from a horse-trapping.* (*Musée de Cluny*)

23 *From a drawing of Sir Geoffrey Luttrell and his wife, in the Luttrell Psalter,*
c. 1340. It shows a horse-trapping and Lady Luttrell wearing a côte-hardie on
which her coat of arms is impaled with that of her husband

Not only did heraldic devices dominate embroidery destined for
the battle-field and occur in ecclesiastical work but during the late
14th century fashion also dictated that a wife should wear upon her
côte-hardie her own coat of arms impaled with that of her hus-
band(23). The simple cut of her graceful dress was a perfect field
for such designs worked in hemmed or couched appliqué, with
detail in couching and outline stitch. Such blazoning is shown on
the brass of 1384 at Southacre, Norfolk, of Sir J. Harsick and his
wife. Sir G. Felbrigge, 1400, at Playford, Suffolk, and P. Gerard,
1492, Winwick, Lincolnshire, have lions rampant on their tabards.
John Wantele, 1424, at Amberley, Sussex, has leopard's masks on
his shirt or surcoat. These clothes must have been both beautiful
and important to have featured upon memorial brasses. The dress
and cloak in which Lady Warwick is depicted, with its delicate
embroidery in lozenge shapes, may have been one of her favourites
since this brass (1406, St. Mary, Warwick) is an example in which
the clothes of husband and wife are unrelated in design.

Royal garments were very elaborate and are fascinating to read about; Kendrick speaks of a white robe embroidered in gold and silk, with branches of broom and rosemary, another powdered with golden squirrels, which would have been as lively in drawing as the lion in the Cluny chasuble; a blue cloth scattered with crescents and stars; a green robe embroidered with pheasant's feathers and many others of equal delicacy and richness. During this period the very extravagant decorations of pearls, jewels and gold thread resulted in the passing of sumptuary laws to restrict their use on clothes.

In the home itself embroidered decoration was as yet limited to wall, partition and bed-hangings, none of which has survived, but we know that their treatment and subject matter were similar to that of clothing of the period, and to the narrative embroidery already mentioned under ecclesiastical work. Clothes and hangings were sometimes bequeathed to monasteries and abbeys to be remodelled into vestments and altar-cloths. Small bags to hang from the girdle were made from fragments, sometimes from ecclesiastical garments and it would be possible for a royal robe to become a chasuble, while the precious pieces left over were made into bags for civilian use. One small seal bag—$5'' \times 4\frac{3}{4}''$—made in the early 14th century and ever since owned by the Corporation of London, was especially to hold a seal, for it is attached to a charter of June 8th 1319. It is worked in cross and split stitch in coloured silks and silver gilt thread on linen, with some couching. There are different heraldic devices on either side with a diagonal grounding in eyelet stitch, which may be unusual at this early date.

The earliest known English embroidered bookbinding belongs to the late 14th century. Called the Felbrigge Psalter, it may have been worked by Anne Felbrigge at this time or made from fragments of an outworn altar-cloth or vestment. In style it belongs to Opus Anglicanum with a background in gold thread, 10 strands to $\frac{1}{8}''$, to form a chevron pattern. There is a crucifixion scene on the back, in which the pose of the Virgin is similar to that upon the Vienna Chasuble(14). It is the forerunner of 16th-century English bindings.

One important secular use of embroidery, which is sometimes overlooked, was the work required by the Livery Companies of the City of London. Their dress was symbolic, an outward sign of brotherhood. In ceremonial functions such as the crowning of new Wardens, or in royal pageants on the Thames, distinguishing features of livery, badges, banners, shields and streamers were essential. Very little of this 15th-century work remains, apart from palls owned by the Fishmongers' Company and the Brewers' Company. The Fishmongers' Company pall has a central panel of red and gold Florentine velvet brocade. The falls are richly embroidered in fine gold and silk showing the arms of the Company supported by mermaids which are worked in silk and metal thread and are earlier than the fabric around which they are mounted.

The Brewers' Company pall is of Florentine cut velvet on cloth of gold. The velvet borders are worked in silver gilt thread and silk and show the Virgin in glory, figures of saints and blazons which include decorative ears of barley.

A Vintners' pall of slightly later date incorporates grapes in its design, and the Merchant Taylors' a lamb and flag. The Ironmongers' Company furnished their hall with a hearse cloth or pall of gold and a suit of vestments of cloth-of-gold and carpets of tapestry work for a table. The Glovers' Company still has an apprentice's cap and the Bakers' Company needlework shields (fenders) to hang over the side of the Company's barge. Numerous Masters' crowns from various guilds still exist. A Broderer's crown of the 16th century is probably typical of those made earlier(24). It is a simple band 3″ wide of crimson velvet, embroidered in slightly raised metal thread and silk with pomegranates, roses and strawberries; it has a badge in the centre, and an inscription inside in Roman lettering, velvet applied to velvet, couched with gold thread.

The need for such work must have helped to keep the craft alive until it was given new life by the demands of Henry VIII.

24   *Master's crown of the Broderers' Company*

Early Tudor

The mediaeval craftsman left behind him a legacy of astonishing beauty. A general decline in skill, however, marked the late 14th and early 15th century in the craft of embroidery, and this must be attributed to the Black Death and importation of Italian brocades already mentioned, combined with the increasingly unsatisfactory conditions in monastic establishments where most of the work not carried out in guild workshops was produced. Nevertheless, by the time of Henry VIII a long and gradual process of recovery had taken place. A final impetus to the revival of the art was given by the dispersal of craftsmen from the monasteries.

This improvement coincided with a change in economic conditions and the widespread redistribution of wealth, for there emerged a new type of countryman, able, if astute, to acquire land, in time to be increased and handed down to his sons; earlier perhaps he had benefited from the French wars and the internal strife of the Wars of the Roses, or had been helped by trade expansion, or had been further enriched by Henry VII from lands forfeit through the Star Chamber law suits. Now the dispersal of monastic land by Henry VIII created a new aristocracy anxious to display their new wealth and power in many ways, one of which was the splendour of their clothes. Costume reached the height of adornment in Elizabeth's reign, but it is not surprising to find that under Henry VIII the emphasis moved away from the requirements of the church.

In the 16th century very little ecclesiastical embroidery was needed and little remains for us to see today. A cope of red velvet and cloth of gold, with a pattern of roses and portcullises, one of a

25 *A cope of red velvet and cloth of gold*

set of vestments woven in Florence for Westminster Abbey, is now at Stonyhurst College(25). An altar frontal (V. & A.) which may have been part of a mid-16th-century funeral pall, shows the kneeling figures of Ralph, fourth Earl of Westmorland (d. 1549) with his seven sons. It is worked in couched gold, silver-gilt and silver giving a variety of textures.

The focus, particularly after the Dissolution of the Monasteries, was upon domestic and ceremonial embroidery. Life in England was slowly yet irrevocably changing to a way not so very different from our own, and we should reconsider the setting in which embroidery is to be used henceforth.

IN THE HOME

Scattered throughout England there are many mediaeval houses, both great and small, which were once owned by merchants who, with the help of their industrious families, enriched their homes. Architecturally we can trace the gradual development from the semi-fortified manor house with its cold stone walls hung with tapestries to the home which combined the strength of earlier reigns with a new quality, that of intimacy. Previously this had been lacking and families had tried to achieve some privacy with tapestry or embroidered partition hangings, the *salle d'Angleterre* of the mediaeval castle.

During the Tudor period the number of rooms increased, and in all of them some embroidery would be found. In the houses of the nobility the rooms were usually still arranged around a quadrangle and the great hall remained an architectural feature, but there could also be a parlour for summer and winter use, a private dining room, and a study. Bedrooms multiplied, at Hengrave Hall, Suffolk, built in 1538, to the alarming total of forty and many would be to us very disconcerting because in larger houses they were used as thoroughfares, making the heavily curtained bed a necessity in a draughty place. Some rooms on the other hand were very small indeed, low-pitched and with tiny windows, even in houses as great as Compton Wynyates in Warwickshire where the majority of rooms are large. They show the contrast between the life of formal entertainment of royalty and ambassadors and the everyday life of the resident family.

In this more settled era the home slowly grew more comfortable.

Furniture was still made of oak and therefore heavy because the wood is very hard with a grain that does not lend itself to delicate workmanship, but it was an excellent foil for the accompanying embroidery. Fourpost beds with carved testers had lined embroidered curtains hanging down to the ground, with a wide valance at the top and a bedspread which also reached to the floor. Such a set of hangings belonging to royalty or for use in a royal guest room would have crowned initials and emblems worked in silk and gold on silk or velvet, or be "paned",[1] and might well have been made either by men and women who had been trained in monastery or abbey or by members of the Broderers' Company. Because the bedroom was also a reception room there might well be loose cushions embroidered for chairs and stools, in gold couched appliqué on velvet or of Turkey work, a form of hand knotted embroidery imitating Turkish carpet weaving. We do not know exactly when Turkey work was introduced, but a piece is mentioned as being old and worn in 1549, so that it probably came very early in the 16th century; while in the parlour the rare carpet, whether embroidered in tent stitch on canvas by a guild or imported from the Levant, covered a long oak table, for it was too valuable to be used on the floor.

CLOTHES

In these surroundings the Tudor noblewoman moved in costume outwardly as graceful as at any period in history. Her dress, with its tightly fitting stiffened bodice and full skirt of satin or velvet or fine home-spun woollen cloth, might have decoration in gold down the skirt or around the hem, perhaps following the fashionable arabesque design upon her husband's doublet. The arabesque, so often used during the Early Tudor period, came from Turkey and the Middle East to Venice, thence to England with the magnificent silks, brocades and velvets made in Venetian workshops. Arabesque

[1] When vertical strips of fabric contrasting either in colour or texture or both are used to widen the range, e.g. plain white silk and white damask or dull green damask and red damask, or damask and velvet, they are said to be paned or paled, a term linked with heraldry—a shield may be parti per pale, i.e. vertically divided.

In a Wolsey inventory "pieces of hangings, paned white and green, with branches of roses, red and white", are mentioned.

This method of extending the use of a limited amount of material was not confined to late mediaeval and Tudor embroidery. At Ham House, Richmond, there are wall-hangings of paned damask and dark blue velvet, with appliqué, worked as late as 1683.

designs were often outlined in gold thread, which together with silk sewing thread was also imported from Venice. To decorate the low square neck of the bodice, a narrow edging of delicate black silk embroidery was worked on fine white linen, matched at the cuffs or there greatly elaborated, in a style now known as Holbein stitch. Similar decorative edgings were made for men's cuffs and narrow ruffs. Such stitchery can be seen in portraits in the National Portrait Gallery, London. Queen Catherine Howard, 1541, has a linen tunic with floral stems in black, with gold arabesques on her dress, and Queen Mary, 1553–8, wears a linen tunic of Holbein stitch worked in red.

Continental styles, mainly French, Spanish and Italian, continued to influence our clothes. In a portrait of Eleanor of Toledo, by Bronzino (Wallace Collection), the embroidery is clearly drawn (26, ₁). Black velvet applied to white satin is held down with gold plaited braid stitch and edged with black couching. Large areas of gold in the design are filled with rows of plaited braid stitch and outlined with black couching. Sleeves and neckline have a very narrow border of cross stitch and double running. Many Tudor women must have worn similar dresses.

A man's costume was at this time more elaborate than a woman's, as we may see in many portraits of Henry VIII, who no doubt set the fashion and saw to it that his clothes outshone all others (26, ₅, ₈). Trunk hose and cloak were embroidered in gold and silk with rich bands of interlacing patterns or arabesques, or a combination of both. Many yards of fabric and hours of strong sewing, many ounces of expensive gold and silk, and in the padded doublets much carded fleece, were needed to dress this virile extravagant monarch and his courtiers[1].

If we were to rely only upon written records we might imagine that clothes worn in the 16th century were not very different from

---

[1] "His Majesty's expenses . . . 16,000 ducats for the wardrobe, for he is the best dressed sovereign in the world." "He is extremely fond of tennis, at which game it is the prettiest thing in the world to see him play, his fair skin glowing through a shirt of the finest texture." (Dispatch of Giustiniani, Venetian Ambassador, Calendar of State Papers, 1519.)

"He (Sir Thomas More) dresses very simply, and wears no silk or purple or gold chains, except when it is impossible to avoid it." (Erasmus' letter to Ulrich von Hulten, 1519.)

"The Queen (Mary Tudor) seems to delight above all in arraying herself elegantly and magnificently." (Giacomo Soranzo, Venetian Ambassador, Venetian State Papers, 1554.)

26 (1) *Design in cross stitch on sleeves and neckline worn by Eleanor of Toledo,*
    1559, in a portrait by Bronzino (Wallace Collection)
    (2) *Holbein stitch border and frill on low neckline in portrait of Margaret*
    Pole, Countess of Salisbury, 1473–1541 (N.P.G.)
    (3) *Jug in silver-gilt. Turkish. 16th century (V. & A.). Such an arabesque*
    design inspired the Tudor embroideress
    (4) *Interlacing arabesque in twisted metal thread with jewels in metal*
    settings upon black velvet, from a portrait of Edward VI, 1537–53, painted
    1550
    (5) *Interlacing arabesque design on Henry VIII's shirt to be seen on a*
    cartoon for a painting in the Privy Chamber, Whitehall, and several of his
    other portraits by Holbein
    (6) *Motif similar to that found on the head-dress of Margaret Roper (d.*
    1544), gold thread on white linen, in portrait of Sir Thomas More and
    descendants (N.P.G.)
    (7) *Motif from Sir Henry Lee's (1530–1610) shirt, black silk on linen, in a*
    portrait by Antonio Mor (N.P.G.)
    (8) *Interlacing strapwork design on the hem and sleeves of a cloak in a*
    portrait of Henry VIII (Liverpool Art Gallery)

---

those of the mediaeval world: "yellow satin embroidered with gold;
black velvet with gold; a purple velvet jerkin with purple satin
sleeves all embroidered in Venice gold; a doublet with silver
arabesques; Spanish work in red on white linen."[1] To avoid this
misconception it is essential that as full use as possible be made of
the fine Tudor portraiture to widen our knowledge: such descrip-
tions should be fitted into that context.

The Tudor artist was always at great pains to record with
detailed accuracy the clothes and jewellery of his subject. Often
thread and stitches are recognisable, whether the design is of
woven brocade or brocade embellished with stitchery. In the
portrait group of Sir Thomas More and his family (N.P.G.) the
women's coifs are of special interest (26, 6).

The Field of the Cloth of Gold, one of the most magnificent and
recklessly extravagant events of all time, is recorded in a large
painting at Hampton Court Palace; together with written records
we are helped to visualise the astonishing amount of work demanded
of guild embroiderers not only for the dress of royalty and nobility
and their retainers, of ecclesiastical dignitaries, of heralds and
gentlemen at arms, but also upon the magnificent banqueting tents
and other accoutrements of hospitality. Though it is far more
probable that the interlacing arabesques shown in the picture were

[1] Kendrick.

painted upon the tents, this is unlikely to be true of the costume. We are told that Henry VIII wore cloth of gold and Francis I satin with gold and purple; both monarchs probably wore waist-length cloaks similar to extant Spanish examples of about the same date, with heavily embroidered bands down the front and continuing round the hem, and shoes with raised soles edged with silver, embroidered in raised gold in a heavily scrolling leaf design on a velvet ground. Nothing else tangible remains of that last great outburst of mediaeval glory which surrounded the two "modern" statesmen at their meeting; but sufficient paintings exist to help us visualise the beauty of this age of personal display.

Elizabethan and Early Stuart

Embroidery in the reign of Queen Elizabeth I burst into flower. Garden and country flowers enclosed in freely scrolling lines appeared on coifs and bodices, on tunics and skirts, on collars and dresses, on men's indoor hats and upon gloves. They flowed over bedspreads and long pillow covers and over cushions, not in any riotous abandon but with great vigour and variety in treatment, exquisite stitchery and sensitive drawing. Ideas came from many sources, certainly not only from nature. The needlewoman's enthusiasm for plant life led her to search through old manuscripts and herbals, while the shrewd French and Italians made drawings and pattern books to be imported especially for her use. Those still in existence are much pricked, often carelessly through several pages, for marking the fabric, and have pages torn out. Gerard's *Herball*, published in 1597, with its clear drawings, must have

(*Continued on page 46*)

---

27   (1), (4) *Motifs taken from two portraits of Queen Elizabeth I* (*National Maritime Museum. Greenwich*)
      (2) *Design from a pattern book published by Richard Shorleyker in 1632, in London*
      (3) *Motif from a portrait of Lady Kitson, 1573* (*Tate Gallery*)
      Insects from various embroideries in the Victoria and Albert Museum

1

2

3

4

fascinated the needlewoman as much in its own time as it does many of us today, but earlier herbals had more influence on Elizabethan design, and the dominating scroll line may even be related to mediaeval tradition. The termination of each sprig or "slip", as if torn from a branch, may derive from these rather than from her aptitude as a gardener(28).

The Elizabethan embroideress even in her more sophisticated work remained a country-woman at heart; English countrypursuits came anachronistically into classical and biblical stories; animals and birds, and not by any means least, a most inventively treated, and fantastic array of worms, caterpillars, spiders, crane-flies, butterflies and unidentifiable insects filled in any available space (27). Space was an ingredient which she did not feel essential to a design, nor was scale of much importance, yet with all this apparent happy inconsequence there is sufficient restraint in colour and a perfect understanding of the limitations of the chosen technique for the work of this period to be amongst the best we have ever produced. Indeed, Elizabethan stitchery at times, with regard to refinement of detail approached the quality of Opus Anglicanum, for instance in the minute speckling which so closely followed the engraved pattern sometimes printed on linen for black work. The needlewoman was greatly assisted in this achievement by the

(Continued on page 48)

---

28   *Motifs from Elizabethan Embroidery*
      (1) *From a red velvet square cushion (V. & A.) worked in silk and variously twisted gold threads, carelessly couched*
      (2) *From a velvet long cushion (V. & A.) in natural colours: cross stitch and tent stitch on canvas which seems to have lost its shape in working, giving a pleasantly irregular result; each motif is secured with two rows of silver-gilt thread*
      (3) *From a woman's jacket (V. & A.) covered with a scrolling design of flowers and fruit in silk in natural colours and metal thread. Two strawberries have gold seeds over silk fillings and one has a red stem stitch outline round a gold thread filling. The strawberry leaves are worked in two shades of green twisted together, a device used to help the limited range of colours available; their veins are pale blue. The seams of this garment are beautifully joined with buttonhole insertion stitch and the edges are embroidered to match* ▶
      (4) *From a woman's jacket (Met. Mus.) in coloured silk and metal thread needlepoint fillings*
      (5) *From a coif (Met. Mus.) in coloured silk needlepoint fillings and silver-gilt plaited braid stitch*

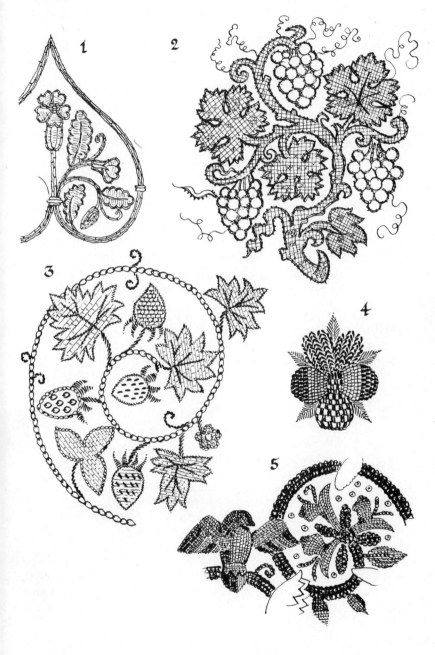

29   (1) *Part of a diaper pattern on a late 16th-century coif; silver-gilt plaited*
      knots and stem stitch
      (2), (3) *16th-century fillings*
      (4) *Design on a black work coif and forehead cloth; late 16th century*
      (6) *Design on falling cape collar mainly in herringbone $\frac{1}{12}''$ wide in black*
      silk on linen
      (5), (8), (9), (10) and (14). *Details of fillings used in* (7)
      (7) *Long cushion cover in black work using back, chain and stem stitch with*
      speckling and many Holbein stitch diaper patterns; in black silk on linen;
      second half 16th century
      (11), (12) *Black work motifs from portraits*
      (13) *Design on bodice worked in chain stitch in silver thread with spangles*
      on the sleeves. 1625–40

---

availability of steel needles which were first made in England in
Queen Elizabeth I's reign. They must have been very fine indeed;
some of the beads and seed pearls then used would require the
thinnest of present-day needles; cylindrical cases covered with
twisted silk and metal thread were made to hold them.

> *A Needle (though it be but small and slender)*
> *Yet it is both a maker and a mender.*[1]

A very fine flexible metal thread called "passing" was known to
the Elizabethans. It was used freely for plaited braid stitch stems and
flower centres; in spots of interlaced knot stitch, chain stitch outlines, buttonhole fillings and work on canvas.

CLOTHES

> *And thus without our Bibs and Biggins bee;*
> *No Shirts or Smockes, our nakednesse to hide,*
> *No Garments gay, to make us magnified:*
> *No Shadows, Shapparoones, Caules, Bands, Ruffs, Kuffs,*
> *No Kerchiefs, Quoyfes, Chin-clouts, or Marry-Muffes,*
> *No Cros-cloaths, Apron, Hand-kerchiefs, or Falls,*
> *No Table-cloathes for Parlours or for Halls,*
> *No Sheets, no Towels, Napkins, Pillow-beares,*
> *Nor any Garment man or woman weares.*

Though not published until 1636, J. Taylor in *The needle's*
Excellency gives us a clear indication of the range of work covered,
a list which would be equally applicable to the preceding eighty
years.

[1] J. Taylor. *The needle's Excellency*, 1636.

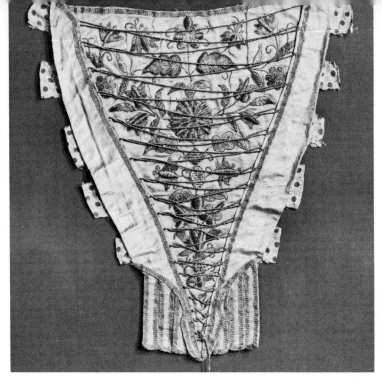

▲ *Stomacher, 1730-50. Pink satin embroidered in green and yellow silk, metal thread and braid; lacing of metal thread. Courtesy of the City of Manchester Art Galleries*

Pockets, 1774. Ribbed linen, embroidered in coloured wools. Courtesy of the City of Manchester Art Galleries
▼

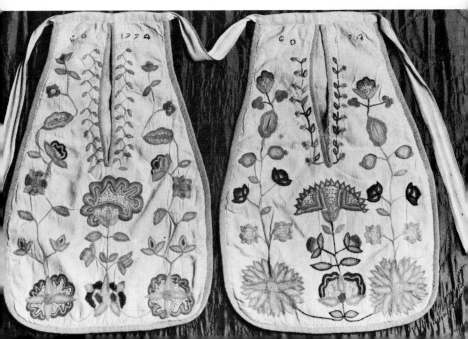

▲ *Cape, 1894-6. Dark fawn cloth with appliqué; circular, with high, shaped collar. Courtesy of the City of Manchester Art Galleries*

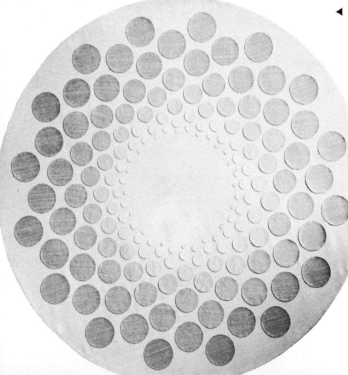

◄ *"Spinning Disc" by Jer̶ Gray. The disc and c̶ on it are of pink-orange̶ Sekers fabric. Their c̶ appears to change as̶ disc spins against a ḇ̶ ground of pink-orange̶ silk. Courtesy of Jer̶ Gray*

BLACK WORK MOTIFS

It is impossible to name the precise moment when scrolling floral designs invaded the feminine wardrobe to take precedence over interlaced strapwork and arabesques; these, though less dominant a feature than in Henry VIII's time, persisted in men's clothes throughout the 16th and well into the 17th century.

Of embroidery methods used on clothes there are at this time three—black work, white work and embroidery in coloured silk—which deserve special study. There was, however, no rigid attitude towards keeping separate the different types of embroidery.

Black Work

Black work is the name given to embroidery in one colour, normally black silk, though occasionally red, as on the linen sleeves and cuffs of Mary I, 1516–58 (N.P.G.). A. J. B. Wace says "It seems to have been known in England before the end of the 15th century." It is a development from Holbein stitch, released in the latter half of the 16th century from the rigidity of the counted thread, though this is observed in the intricate diaper patterns used as filling stitches(29). Freely scrolling stems, worked in plaited braid stitch in silver and silver-gilt thread or closely worked braid stitch in black silk enclose flower and leaf motifs which are worked in a variety of stitches, or with microscopic black silk speckling, a stitch at this time only found in black work. The stitches used include chain, back, sword, Pekinese, buttonhole, coral, closed herringbone, braid, plaited braid and speckling. Tiny silver spangles, rings of wire hammered flat, smaller than the present day sequin, fastened with a French knot, fill up empty spaces. The embroidery is always worked upon fine linen or cambric. The apparently severe limitations of black, gold and silver in no way deterred the Elizabethan needlewoman from creating a great variety of designs based almost entirely upon the scroll and diaper pattern; it would appear that the limitation itself was a stimulus to invention.

White Work

White work is much heavier in style in the late 16th and early 17th centuries than it is two hundred years later when it again becomes fashionable. Designs repeat regularly but are not usually based upon a simple scroll. Drawn threadwork fillings and reticella motifs are combined in highly conventional leaves and flowers. If the work was partially quilted the design was worked in back stitch through two thicknesses of linen; the part to be quilted was padded from behind and the second fabric removed to allow drawn fabric stitches to be embroidered. Further variation in light and shade came from the use of flat stitch, from completely filling some areas with French knots, by outlining with fine cord, and the judicious placing of silver-gilt thread on flower centres, petals or even stems.

Work in Coloured Silk

Embroidery in coloured silk is seldom used without metal thread. Scrolling stems enclose plant forms worked in colour chosen with some slight regard for nature; buttonhole stitch fillings play a very large part in the treatment of the design but a variety of other stitches is found including stem, chain, herringbone, basket filling, bullion knots, long and short, and plaited braid. Where detached buttonhole fillings are used they form an historic link with 17th-century "stump work".[1]

From the various unfinished examples we can see the usual working method—the design was either pricked and pounced and drawn with a clear black line, or it was printed from an engraving

[1] Colours of silk thread: "royal blue, pale blue, grass green, pale green, cream, bright yellow, pink and carmine or crimson. Rarer colours are purple, dark green, olive, yellow-brown, sepia, salmon-pink, pale vermilion (flame colour) and shades of reddish mauve; minor shades are sometimes produced by wrapping two strands of silk, e.g. red and white to produce pink."—Nevinson.

30 *In an Italian pattern book*, Giardineto novo di Punto, *published in Venice in 1566, the designs become progressively more difficult from page one, on which* ¼" *borders are composed of one or two motifs, to the final few pages of seemingly complicated all-over designs, yet these too are based on motifs given earlier in the book. Most designs are geometric but there are a few human figures, birds, plants, urns, fleurs-de-lis and one border using the arabesque. Two ABC's are included of Roman lettering, such as may be found on 17th-century white work samplers. Several pages have designs for shirt openings, giving a practical use for borders three or four squares wide*

direct upon the linen, a method which allowed much more detail and even shows the position of the speckling (V. & A.).

Shorleyker, in his pattern book *A Scholehouse for the Needle* (27, ₂), published in 1632, includes under "cut-workes", edgings, insertions, interlacing, strapwork, arabesque designs similar to those on Persian copper vessels, not very accurate counted satin stitch, various needlepoint lace designs, not all of them geometric, for mermaids, angels, the Pelican in her Piety and the Evangelists are also used. There are drawings of birds, a bat, reptiles and insects, many of which have been pricked, some carelessly through several pages and others are smudged where charcoal has been pounced through. Also included is the potato flower, then a novelty. To help the needlewoman even further he says, in explanation of a page of squares drawn to two sizes:

> I would have you know, that the use of these squares doth showe how you may continue any worke, Bird, Beast, or Flower: into bigger or lesser proportions, according as you shall see cause: As thus if, you will enlarge your patterne, devide it into squares: then rule a paper as large as ye list, into what squares you will: Then looke how many holes your patterne doth containe, upon so many holes of your ruled paper drawe your patterne.

MEN'S CLOTHES

The Elizabethan merchant was richly clothed—the courtier more elaborately attired. Common to both were the padded doublet, linen shirt, short cloak, trunk hose, canions (thigh covering between knee and trunk hose), out-door hat and indoor cap; nor was embroidery on handkerchiefs, gloves, stockings and shoes disregarded.

Cloaks, Doublets, Hose

The tendency, noted earlier, was for narrow striped all-over designs of interlacing, of arabesques or of small motifs arranged diagonally on doublets, cloaks and trunk hose. These garments were made of silk, satin or velvet and worked in silk and much purl and couched metal thread, some of which was slightly padded and raised. A man's waist length velvet cloak in the London Museum has a border about 4″ wide of scrolling arabesques in raised metal thread. A portrait of Sir Christopher Hatton painted in 1575 shows on his canions a design using strapwork and conventional plant form; on another portrait, of Sir Philip Sydney (N.P.G.), the design on his trunk hose is entirely of strapwork.

Shirts

On shirts, the trend is gradually away from the Holbein stitch of Henry VIII's reign towards white work by the time of Charles I. Charles I's shirt (London Museum), is of fine white linen richly sewn along the hem and down both sides of each seam with drawn thread work and bands of needlepoint lace. There is a wider band of embroidery between elbow and wrist with small red and blue ribbon bows. Green and gold cord is added at the wrists. The neckband is narrow but elaborately stitched in needlepoint. Other shirts in private collections, worn by Charles I, have four-sided stitch and eyelet stitch on the front opening, French knots and double back stitch and some rudimentary smocking above the wrist bands. A woman's nightdress, about 1590 (London Museum), has bands of needlepoint lace at the hem and on the collar and cuffs and down the front opening.

It is difficult to distinguish between men's and women's shirts and nightdresses; both are treated similarly, open from throat to chest.

Collars

Collars in boldly designed black work, edged with reticella lace are to be seen in portraits(32) and of Henry, Lord Winsor, painted in 1588 (Oakley Park), and John Bull painted in 1589 (Faculty of Music, Oxford).

Italian needlepoint or reticella lace was a very distinctive feature of a man's costume. It was worn in large quantities at neck and

31   *Ruff worn by Sir Edward Hoby*
in his portrait, 16th century

32   *Design from a collar, which has cuffs to*
match, in a portrait painted in 1589 of Sir
Christopher Hatton (N.P.G.). The edge is of
reticella lace

wrist and appears to have fascinated
every contemporary portrait painter.
It is recorded so faithfully that there
would be no difficulty in reproducing
many of the designs. Indeed, stitchery,
whether in silk or metal thread, is in
many paintings clearly recognisable.

Caps

Men's informal day caps, erroneously called night-caps, have survived fairly well, perhaps because it was difficult to turn them into
anything else, or because they tucked away easily into a drawer.
They are uniformly charming, diverse in treatment. They can be
found today in museums in England and U.S.A. and in many
private collections. All, like that worn by Phineas Pett for his
portrait painted in 1613 (N.P.G.), are made of one strip partly cut
into four points shaped to meet at the crown, with the lower edge
turned back to form a cuff. Phineas Pett's cap is decorated with a

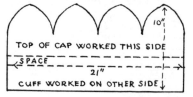

33   *16th-century man's cap worked entirely in silver-gilt and silver thread on*
linen in chain and plaited braid stitch. The same design might well have been
worked in coloured silks

scrolling design in silk, of red flowers and dark green leaves, and is embellished with gold thread, gold lace and spangles.

A man's linen cap, late 16th or early 17th century (London Museum) is entirely in silver and silver-gilt thread with closely scrolling stems bearing highly raised thistles and slightly raised pansies; many gold spangles cover the small amount of linen that might otherwise show between them(33).

WOMEN'S CLOTHES

We may judge the style of women's clothes from effigies, pictures and inventories. Queen Elizabeth I's vanity is well known and her wardrobe vast to satisfy one aspect of her nature—many of her portraits testify to the richness of invention, wealth of jewels and the phenomenal quantity of pearls then in use. Some allowance must be made for flattery—not to have done so would have jeopardised not only the painter's career but his life—but enough clothes remain for us to see that even those of the noblewoman were very beautiful; how much more so must have been those of the Queen.

Every part of a woman's clothing was embroidered: full skirt, sometimes opened in front to show the petticoat, bodice (jacket or tunic), deep stomacher, yoke, sleeves, ruff, cuffs, coif and triangular forehead cloth, and hoods worn by elderly women, large falling collars, handkerchief, slippers, chemise and nightgown. There was apparently a tendency to embroider such parts as would show and to tack them to the main garment, which would explain references to pairs of sleeves and some curious, almost oval sleeve pieces which were evidently set into 14″ slashes, lengthwise from upper arm past the elbow in bodices and doublets; yokes and stomachers were likewise detachable.

In one of the many portraits of Queen Elizabeth I, arabesques, strapwork and flowers intermingle upon her dress(34), but the

34   *Decoration repeated down the buttoned front opening of a tunic worn by Queen Elizabeth I in a portrait (N.P.G.). Treatment suggests that gold and silver thread are worked on red velvet*

scrolling floral design is so characteristic a feature that after a study of 16th and early 17th century work we should automatically assign it to this era. Garden flowers, rose, cornflower, borage, pansy, crown imperial lily, columbine, daffodil, carnation; wild flowers, thistle, convolvulus, honeysuckle, foxglove, daisy; fruit and berried plants, pear, nut, pomegranate, strawberry, grape, acorn; the peascod, transparent or open to show the peas, raindrops, birds, and animals are but a few from a large repertoire freely used with the scroll. Similarity in fruit and flower designs all over England suggests some easily accessible source. Even if the same motif in a different guise can be found again and again, there was versatility in subject matter which increased towards the end of the century and is stressed in *The needle's Excellency*:

> *Flowers, Plants, and Fishes, Beasts, Birds, Flyes, and Bees,*
> *Hils, Dales, Plaines, Pastures, Skies, Seas, Rivers, Trees;*
> *There's nothing neare at hand, or farthest sought,*
> *But with the Needle may be shap'd and wrought.*

Jackets, Stomachers, Sleeves, Yokes

The majority of extant linen jackets are closely covered with a scrolling floral design in meticulously detailed black work or in buttonhole fillings in coloured silks and metal thread. The sparkle of silk and silver-gilt made gay apparel. Such a tunic worn by Margaret Laton for her portrait still exists, and it is interesting to compare the two, observing the accuracy of the painted record. A blouse (Whitworth Art Gallery, Manchester) is designed in horizontal bands with clouds and raindrops amongst other devices and still retains, largely intact, the original buttonhole insertion stitch on the seams. Portraits of Queen Elizabeth I indicate that on jackets a wide range of designs existed.

A portrait of Mary Queen of Scots (N.P.G.) shows a yoke which may be either white work or black work. Stomachers and sleeves were similarly treated. Plaited braid stitch in metal thread is a distinctive feature of the period.

Coifs, Forehead Cloths

Women's linen coifs, which like men's caps are fairly numerous, were embroidered in black work, white work, and in coloured silks; all these methods were used either alone(37) or with metal thread(35). Diaper patterns tend to be used only for black work and more elaborately constructed designs occur in white work, but in all three methods the scroll line is most usual, each scroll containing a flower or leaf.

The area of a coif before it is made up is only about $20'' \times 9''$. Within this small space, and keeping to the convention of the time,

35   *Black work coif*, c. *1600 (V. & A.). Scrolling design using pea, rose, pink foxglove, strawberry, cornflower, pear, columbine, violet, solanum, and imaginary flowers. Stems are in silver-gilt, outlined with black; flower centres and some petals also in silver-gilt; chain stitch, couched work and speckling are also used.*

  (A) From a different coif in which all motifs are outlined in chain stitch, filled with plaited braid stitch and plaited knots in silver-gilt, and couched work

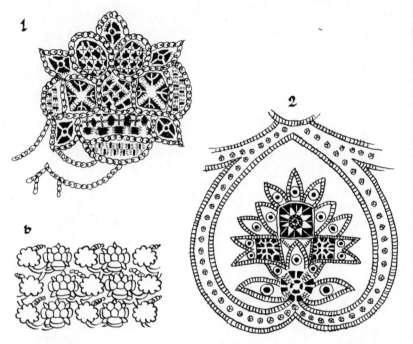

36 *Motifs from late 16th-century white work coifs.*
(1) Outlined in gilt chain stitch; cut and drawn work and needlepoint
fillings on linen. (b) arrangement of all-over pattern
(2) Outlined in ladder stitch; worked in linen thread on linen with French
knots, cut work and needlepoint

the fashionable lady experimented with
her needle(36). A pattern which may in
one coif be outlined in chain stitch in
silver-gilt thread with cut and drawn work
and needlepoint fillings in the leaves, in
another may have the entire background
covered with gold buttonhole stitch, or the
background can be filled with spangles;
the motifs may be outlined with silver-
gilt chain stitch or have a narrow black
outline, or heavy white chain stitch. A
similar design could be entirely in metal
thread, or in coloured silks. In fact

37 *A white work coif*
which has a matching tri-
angular forehead cloth
(V. & A.)

there must have been innumerable variations beyond those we know.

A forehead cloth was triangular, and made to match the coif, over which it was worn.

Petticoats

No Elizabethan petticoats exist. If we are to judge their quality from Queen Elizabeth's portraits the large surface could become the field for most fanciful work and the comment made some years later, in another context, that of a "neat historical shirt", is sufficiently apt to be quoted here:

> My smock sleeves have such holy embroideries
> And are so learned, that I fear in time
> All my apparel will be quoted by
> Some pure instructor.[1]

Yet it is probable that the average design followed more closely the style of a very lovely blue satin petticoat, 3′ 3″ × 8′ 9″, worked entirely in silver-gilt and silver; in a triple scrolling band which extends the whole length, leaves and flowers alternate; above, in the centre, are grouped many different kindred sprays(58). Two placket holes give access to tie-on waist-pockets then in use. This is an exceptionally fine specimen which in style belongs as closely to the beginning as the end of the 17th century when it was worked.

Baby Clothes

Babies, even in poor families, had in the 16th century a large supply of linen including bonnets, scarves, jackets, separate sleeves, bibs, handkerchiefs and mittens. On older children, the linen pinafore was pinned to the front of the dress, hence the name. Designs were very probably similar to those of the late 17th century(60).

ACCESSORIES

Purses or Small Bags

It is a little strange that the Elizabethan woman's ingenuity did not extend to the development of a pocket in any of her clothes. There are so many small bags in private possession as well as in museums, that the original 16th-century output must have been prodigious.

[1] Beaumont and Fletcher, *Custom of the Country.*

Their generally good state of preservation implies that they seldom saw hard use. Fine canvas or linen, four or five inches square is covered entirely with silk and metal thread, and evidently the purse was not expected to take the place of a present day handbag (38, $_3$). As with similar mediaeval bags they probably held only a

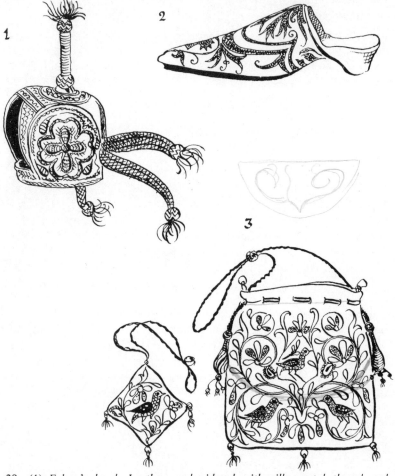

38   (1) *Falcon's hood. Leather, embroidered with silk, metal thread and bullions. 1590–1610*
     (2) *Shoe, blue satin with silver thread. First quarter 17th century*
     (3) *Purse and pin-cushion. Olive green satin, embroidered in gold, with pearls. About 1600*

seal or charm, counters or dice, perfume or pot-pourri if the owner did not possess instead a silver pomander, and may have been intended to hold a New Year gift of money or jewellery. Some of these little bags are very charming with a formal design of flowers and leaves worked in tent stitch which had suddenly become popular, carefully shaded, in coloured silk, against a background of plaited Gobelin stitch in silver thread. Some flowers have petals worked in detached buttonhole stitch which stand away from the main surface. Where stems are part of the design they are in

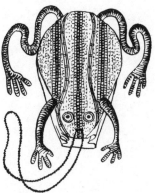

39 *Frog purse; about 2½" long. Worked in silk and a little gold; gussets of oyster silk. 17th century*

raised plaited braid stitch in silver or silver-gilt thread. The bags were lined with coloured silk, closed by draw strings, embellished with groups of tassels and hung from a long cord, all made with plaited metal thread. A matching pin-cushion was not an unusual attachment.

There is a picture in the National Portrait Gallery of Nicholas Bacon (Lord Keeper 1558–79) with his ceremonial purse which appears to be worked in raised gold with small pearls or spangles on red velvet and bears a coat of arms supported by a lion and a griffin.

Not all were regarded with such solemnity—the frog purse(39) is a beautifully embroidered conceit.

Gloves

Late 16th and early 17th century gloves were for ornament rather than use (40). If worn their elaborate gauntlets would not have shown up against the lace or embroidered ruffles at the wrist. They were frequently presented as New Year gifts. The Universities of Oxford and Cambridge[1] both paid homage with embroidered gloves when visited during one of her progresses by Queen Elizabeth I. All have the hand of doe skin with devices to elongate the fingers. Gauntlets are of silk or satin worked in coloured silk,

[1] Nichol, *Progress of Queen Elizabeth.*

silver or silver-gilt thread, and purl; spangles and gold lace, and often seed pearls are included to give a lighter tone. Gloves with tabbed gauntlets, round or square, with a design in each are probably earlier than those in which the gauntlet is slit down one side with the design taken all round as a border; this side opening often has two or three tabs inset. Exact dating of either style is difficult. Several other variations exist; in one sharply pointed triangles contain conventionalised motifs, and another variation is the

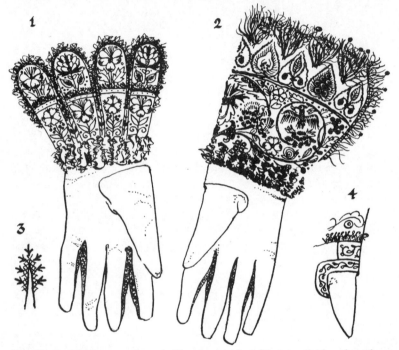

40   (1) *A ruched rose-coloured silk edged with gold gimp divides glove from gauntlet at the wrist. Flowers in natural colours, chiefly pinks, blues and greens are worked on a white satin ground. The hand is thin pale buff leather. About 12″ long*
(2) *This shape gauntlet is often accompanied by three tabs set in the side opening. Here coloured silks are used with raised metal thread and a spangled fringe*
(3) *Detail from one of Charles II's gloves; a device to elongate the fingers with decoration extending down the back of the hand. Seams can be stitched with herringbone or plaited braid stitch in silk or metal thread*
(4) *When the base of the thumb is embroidered a small panel often connects the design with the gauntlet*

mitten, with velvet hand and embroidery spilling on to it from the gauntlet (V. & A.). A few pairs are in existence which have leather gauntlets pierced between the embroidery to give an open work effect a little reminiscent of cut work. The use of black work is very rare indeed. Gloves were seldom decorated after the end of the 17th century; those that do occur are usually wholly of doeskin with a little silk embroidery worked directly upon the leather.

A 17th-century glove-case in the London Museum made from an Elizabethan coif, has heavy silver spirals upon a spangled background, with flowers and birds in coloured silk.

Handkerchiefs

Handkerchiefs were large, for adornment only, made of linen with a wide border of Holbein stitch or Assisi work, in one colour, black, red or blue silk and occasionally a little metal thread. The designs were strongly influenced by Italian pattern books and handkerchiefs from Italy. These included small rectangles of reticella work, bullion knots and either a gold lace or reticella lace edge(41).

The Elizabethan styles of embroidery upon clothes continued well into the 17th century, until the preference for plain silk and satin asserted itself in the reign of Charles I.

ELIZABETHAN HOME

In the Elizabethan home the most important embroidery appeared on table carpets, cushions, long pillows, bed-coverlets, bed-hangings and

41 *Part of a border worked in silk in back, double running and buttonhole stitch on a silk handkerchief, edged with silver-gilt bobbin lace*

valances, wall-hangings and decorative panels. Training in embroidery was part of every girl's upbringing so that in a large household there were many capable trained hands. Even so it must often have been necessary to employ an itinerant designer to draw the designs upon the fabric, for this lengthy task was not something to be done piecemeal. While most household embroidery was made in the home where it was used, large ambitious pieces of work such as the Gifford and Bradford table carpets (V. & A.) probably came from guild workshops.[1]

Table Carpets

Table carpets were worked in several ways. A red velvet carpet (V. & A.) has an all-over pattern of small floral sprigs and a border of larger sprays, all in couched silver and silver-gilt thread and bullions. This is a warm, rich piece of work but the ground fabric of most extant carpets, probably because more enduring, is canvas which is worked with long armed cross, tent and cross stitch in either silk or wool or both threads.

The Gifford carpet (mid-16th century, 18′×4′ 8″) (V. & A.), is worked in tent stitch, in wool, and has in the centre, superimposed upon an intricate geometric pattern, three medallions, one containing the Gifford arms within a floral wreath; the border is narrow and uninspired.

The St. John of Bletso carpet (13′ 9″×6′ 9″) (V. & A.), worked in wool, silk and silver thread, in tent and some cross stitch on canvas, has a scrolling, almost symmetrical design of flowers and fruit on a blue ground. The borders are even more interesting for they contain no less than 20 coats of arms between entwining honeysuckle, vine and flowers on a dark background. In spite of its size it is easy to imagine this being the product of a household, for it is not technically perfect and took several years to complete.

The Bradford carpet (13′×5′ 9″) (V. & A.), is in silk tent stitch on canvas(42). As in the Gifford carpet this has about 400 stitches to the square inch. A competently worked all-over pattern of bunches of grapes covers the flat surface of the table, but the real distinction lies in the wide borders. The design on opposite sides is identical but colour, tone and decorative treatment are different and this is not due to fading. Is it possible that after the tedious vine pattern had been finished in a guild workshop it was sent home to be finished with evident enjoyment by the household? Was insufficient silk dyed to make both sides alike, or did the many ladies stitching away together, invent as they progressed, without too much reference to their companions on the opposite side of

[1] The Broderers were formally incorporated in 1561, but are thought to have existed at least 300 years earlier; all their documents were destroyed in the Great Fire of 1666.

Apparel of an Alb (1320-40), "Annunciation to the Shepherds". Velvet embroidered with coloured silks, silver-gilt and silver thread; in split stitch, underside couching, laid and couched work, and raised work. Victoria and Albert Museum, Crown Copyright

Woman's linen tunic, second half 16th century. Embroidered in coloured silks and metal thread in a scrolling design, with flowers, birds and caterpillars. A needlepoint lace collar has been placed across the shoulders. Victoria and Albert Museum, Crown Copyright

the table? Whatever happened they left behind a dignified and amusing record in a wide pictorial border devoted to scenes from Elizabethan country life. Much action is compressed within a little space. Upon the turbulent waters of a pond a goose and goslings swim, while a large fish is being hooked from amongst them upon the line of a fisher-

42   *From the Bradford table carpet*

man who in turn is in danger from the gun of a wild-fowler aiming at a heron on the bank. We are shown a boar hunt in progress, hounds in pursuit of hare and deer, dogs rabbitting, the village church, farmhouse, great mansion, the mill with its water wheel and a man carrying a sack of flour to be ground. Oaks are laden with acorns, filberts and fruit trees flourish. The Lord and Lady of the Manor are there to survey the scene of perfection.

Cushions

Cushions (43, 47) were made not only for chairs and window seats for human comfort but also for a book, Bible or coronet to rest upon, since these if encrusted with jewels in metal settings would need to be separated from any hard surface. Bible cushions were in daily use at family prayers; an example, $8\frac{1}{2}'' \times 13\frac{1}{2}''$, in silk tent stitch on canvas, depicts "Moses in the bullrushes". These smaller cushions whether of velvet or fine canvas worked with silk or metal thread have appropriate themes. Oblong cushions for chair, stool, or window seat are generally large, about $22''$ wide $\times 3'$ $6''$ long; the width controlled by that of the fabric. They were worked in a frame, and paper was tacked over each part as it was completed.

If on a canvas ground, they are embroidered in cross stitch and tent stitch, mainly in wool, with a little detail in silk. The subject matter of these cushions often includes a coat of arms set among

43   *Design on the back of an X chair
in a portrait of Mary I, painted in 1553;
gold on velvet, showing the use of conventionalised foliage and strapwork.
Upholstered X chair with appliqué of
cloth of gold on a red satin ground.
About 1605. Knole, Kent*

formal flowers and leaves (47, ₁). A very beautiful long cushion can
be seen in the Victoria and Albert Museum. It is on a ground of
black velvet with applied motifs of linen canvas worked in silk.
Thirteen different sprigs, using columbine, pink, marigold, rose,
campion, daffodil, and vine are immediately recognisable (28, ₂).
In the spaces between, regardless of size, are the lion and unicorn,
an elephant, an owl and a parrot, rabbit, cock, hare, dog, and
various strange beasts. These are outnumbered by a glorious
assembly of 12 gnats and 25 centipedes, all exquisitely drawn (44).
It was worked in silk, silver and silver-gilt thread in tent stitch
with additional couching, stem stitch, cross stitch and laid-work.
   Another cushion with appliqué motifs upon white satin makes
some pretence at being a woodland scene (47, ₆). Three trees,
quince, cherry, and orange dominate the design; they are worked
in tent stitch in fairly coarse silk on canvas which was slightly
padded when applied; they are separated by a large thistle and

cornflower plant. A mounted huntsman blowing his horn follows a hound which chases a stag almost beneath the prancing horse of a falconer. Men and women are busy with country pursuits. Many small animals, a turkey and a peacock and the usual insects and spangles prevent any space from appearing neglected. On this cushion only the insects are worked direct upon the satin. When described, these cushions may well sound hopelessly confused, but the sound sense of colour, fine drawing and really inventive

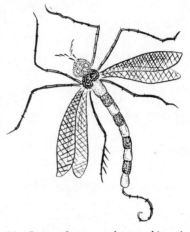

44 *Insect from a velvet cushion, in silk stem stitch, irregularly worked closed herringbone and couched silver-gilt thread*

45 *Flower motif from a satin cushion cover, second quarter 17th century, worked in a scrolling design with daisy, thistle and strawberry in coloured silks in long and short stitch; stems, veins and petal edges are couched with silver-gilt; the background is closely spangled. In both design and method this cushion shows the transition from Elizabethan to Georgian ideas. (Detroit Institute of Arts)*
46 *Detail from late 16th-century pillow or cushion cover worked in silk and gold thread on linen canvas in tent stitch. The background is in Hungarian point. Size 28″ × 21½″*

use of a few simple stitches, create work of vigour and very great charm.

Not all cushions are pictorial; some adhere to the closely scrolling style, worked in coloured silks with a flower head within each scroll, as so often seen in coifs and bodices(45).

An elaborate cushion in metal thread and coloured silks has a tightly scrolled all-over design with a different flower in each scroll(46). Plaited braid stitch in metal thread and buttonhole (needlepoint) fillings predominate in coloured cushions, with back, stem, satin, coral, chain stitch for variety. Other cushions, about

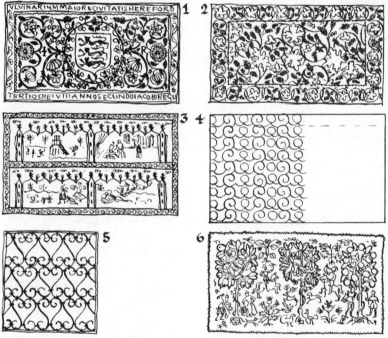

47   *Cushions in the Victoria and Albert Museum showing some of the diverse styles of the 16th and early 17th century*
    (1) *Silk on linen canvas; tent stitch; 42″ × 22″; dated 1604*
    (2) *Black work design in silk on linen; 43″ × 19″*
    (3) *Silk and silver-gilt thread on linen; stem, chain, back and cross stitches with fillings and speckling; 35½″ × 20″*
    (4) *Silk and silver-gilt thread on linen; 35¼″ × 21½″. Diagram of scrolling arrangement*
    (5) *Silk, silver-gilt thread and metal strips on red satin; 20″ × 19″*
    (6) *Motifs in silk and silver thread on canvas applied to linen; 41″ × 22″*

20" square, were worked either on canvas in cross stitch, long-armed cross, or tent stitch, or on satin with couched gold thread, satin stitch and couched work (47, $_5$). Turkey work was also used.

The backs of these cushions, never embroidered, were always of some other material.

With the spread of upholstery early in the next century, loose cushions were rarely made.

Long Pillow-covers

Long pillows and long cushions are the same shape and size (47, $_2$). Cushions were made for the living rooms while pillows formed part of the bed furnishing. They were always made of linen worked in silk. The famous Falkland cushion (V. & A.), often reproduced, is entirely in black silk. In a panel within a scrolling border, it has a freely scrolling design of grapes and vine leaves, each leaf worked with a different diaper pattern in Holbein stitch.

Another, privately owned, equally fine, but with a less lively feeling for the scroll line, far surpasses the Falkland cushion in the inventiveness of its black work diaper patterns which are different in each of its 36 leaves (29, $_7$).

A second style is illustrative; the Victoria and Albert Museum has a set of four pillows worked in dull crimson and dark blue silk; the stories are biblical with the characters in contemporary court costume. The stitches used include decorative fillings, stem, chain, back, cross and speckling (47, $_3$).

Another piece of work, which may have been intended for a cushion, exists in a private collection. This is of interest in that it has no fewer than 72 different plants, each designed to fit a rectangle and embroidered so closely together as to suggest it was not intended to be cut up and the motifs mounted elsewhere; these are arranged eight across and nine down; the use of this embroidery remains conjectural.

Bed-furnishings

The bed was undoubtedly the most comfortable piece of furniture in the house and the bedroom was sometimes a reception room. The Great Bed of Ware, of such outrageous proportions by present-day standards, was not in its own time so unusual; royal beds 11' square existed at Hampton Court.

The bedhead was decorated with a panel of embroidery or tapestry; curtains hung from the tester to the ground and from the tester rail or cornice there were deep valances. With all these to be made for each important bed, together with a counterpane and embroidered bolster with matching pillows for day use, the Elizabethan noblewoman must at times have been sorely in need of many more willing hands than could be mustered from her numerous relatives and servants.

Valances and Bed Hangings

Valances were normally in sets of three, explained by the shape of the Elizabethan bed. They were stretched tightly thus giving a space well adapted to pictorial subjects, which were usually worked in tent stitch on canvas in wool with a little silk detail. Since scriptural and mythological stories received identical treatment, with the characters in court costume in a garden or landscape, it is not always easy to discover to which group the story belongs, and even the story of Rehoboam can be an excellent source of information for 16th-century costume.

The designs are extremely detailed but not at all naturalistic. Colour is limited to shades of blue, green and yellow, with a little red now faded to pale brown. There are, however, examples in the Metropolitan Museum, of two other methods; the first has floral sprays worked in tent stitch on canvas arranged within a geometric strapwork design and applied to violet satin with a couched silver-gilt thread; this late 16th-century valance measures $20'' \times 88''$, incomplete. The second (early 17th century; $8\frac{1}{2}'' \times 108''$) has upon a ground of white and silver ribbed silk, an applied design partly padded, worked in coloured silk, silver and silver-gilt thread and bullion, chiefly in varieties of couching, in an arcaded design with plant forms. Both layouts are reminiscent of mediaeval work.

The important set of green velvet hangings at Oxburgh Hall, Norfolk, includes a coverlet, two curtains, a valance and a number of panels to be applied. The coverlet has 37 canvas-work panels of various creatures, some fabulous and emblematical, with labels in coloured silks, the areas between them broken by a scroll line in gold thread.

A set of equal importance known as the Lochleven hangings, now in the Royal Scottish Museum, Edinburgh, is in black velvet

48   *The Lochleven bed hangings*

appliqué on bright cherry coloured woollen cloth (48). The design is mainly of conventionalised pomegranates, roses and carnations; similar motifs appear in the valance and borders. The embroidery consists partly of applied black velvet, outlined with gold silk cord, and partly of basket stitch over padding, in gold silk laid as if it were metal thread; stems are of blue cord with a thicker strand of gold on each side; elsewhere two shades of gold silk and a little blue, in satin stitch, are used. The very small amount of blue gives an unexpected brilliance to the colour scheme. Only velvet is applied, all other stitchery is direct upon the cloth. There are numerous pieces of embroidery traditionally recorded as the work of Mary Queen of Scots; of these the Lochleven hangings are certainly associated with her household but there is no proof that they are her handiwork. The design shows French and Spanish influence. A similar set of curtains once probably belonged to Linlithgow Palace.

Long Covers or Cupboard Cloths

Several larger pieces of embroidery, similar in material and technique to the pillows, are in existence. Their use is conjectural, for they are too frail for clothing and too thin for curtains. It is thought that they may have been hung over cupboards.

A Stuart will (1622–3) distinguishes between "cupboard carpets" and Turkey work carpets for long tables. One piece 8′ 3¾″ ×19½″ (V. & A.) of great charm, is worked in a wide range of coloured silks, silver, and silver-gilt thread, on linen. Its pattern, of alternating trees and animals, repeats every fourth row. An unworked ink line shows where it was intended to enclose each motif within a scroll. Some leaves and all the animals have unusual fillings. Once again the Elizabethan embroideress shows what she can do with very few stitches, here using only stem, chain, buttonhole, herringbone and plaited braid stitch and couched work.

A second long cover (V. & A.) has a scrolling design of conventionalised flowers, fruit, and leaves with plaited braid stitch in silver-gilt thread, black work diapers and buttonhole fillings.

A far more unusual effect can be seen on the cover, now on loan to the Castle Museum, Nottingham, which is worked in pale shades of coloured silk in chain, satin and back stitch with couched work and French knots on linen. The area, 41″ ×35″, is broken into five wide and six narrow bands, the latter scrolling and the former filled with a great assortment of plant, animal, insect, bird, reptile and marine life, only a few of them repeated and never within the same panel. The following numbers are representative: 10 flowers, 3 birds, 4 fishes, 1 shell, 4 beasts, 1 reptile, 4 large and 23 small insects, and 41 little beetles scattered as if sequins. It has been suggested that this embroidery was intended not for a long cover but to be the back and front of a long pillow made in one piece.

Large Decorative Panels

Lofty state rooms in great houses were still hung with mediaeval tapestries, and the wish to bring colour to the wooden panelling of smaller rooms is evident in the creation of embroideries in tent stitch on canvas to simulate tapestry and anticipating embroidered pictures of the second half of the 17th century. A panel in the Victoria and Albert Museum, about 4′ ×5′, is in tent stitch, has pear, apple and pine trees, flamingo, hoopoe and other identifiable birds in unusually drab greens and browns and could at a little distance easily be mistaken for a woven hanging. Others, more obviously influenced by Indian "palimpores",[1] are designed around the palm tree with monkeys, toucans and exotic flowers, while those at Hardwick Hall may be regarded as more typical.

Embroidery at Hardwick Hall

One great house in particular, Hardwick Hall, Derbyshire, merits separate treatment. Here a phenomenal amount of embroidery was produced, owing to the enthusiasm of an exceptionally forceful personality, that of the Countess of Shrewsbury, better known as "Bess of Hardwick". Her son, travelling in the Far East, sent home examples of work, including a Persian bed quilt and coverlet, but these appear to have had very little effect on her designs which, with the exception of one set of wall-hangings, are wholly English in outlook. This set, each panel 12' high, on a black velvet ground, shows strong classical influence in the architectural settings and Roman lettering inscriptions. The subject matter is largely concerned with the personification of the Virtues and Vices, the Sciences and various emblematic devices whose significance is no longer completely understood. Incorporated in the panels are 30 fragments of copes which came into the family's possession at the Dissolution of the Monasteries. Other hangings with more indigenous subject matter show an experimental attitude towards the craft and control of materials born of considerable technical knowledge, for example a "panel of patchwork velvet with circular medallions containing designs outlined in black silk thread and tinted brown, apparently by singeing" (Jourdain). A variation, again in an interlacing strapwork design, was to cut away the pile of green velvet, leaving the strapwork in relief, outlined with yellow silk cord. A third treatment of strapwork $(49, {}_1)$ shows a 16" square of velvet with a design in pale coloured satin applied to it by means of an outline of gold thread; the rest of the embroidery is in appliqué and coloured silks. It bears the monogram of Elizabeth, Countess of Shrewsbury.

A large set of octagonal panels 14" in diameter worked in tent stitch, with devices from herbals, enclosed in an inscribed border, appears not to have been used until mounted in the early 20th

[1] Printed cotton bedspreads.

century. They may have been intended for use, scattered upon a velvet ground as in the work at Oxburgh Hall.

"Bess" and her ladies also completed several tent stitch hangings, each about 25″ × 50″, in silk and wool, of classical and biblical subjects, the main interest in which lies in the accurate representation of Elizabethan costume—but the Hardwick embroideries, though numerous and competent, are neither outstandingly beautiful in colour nor imbued with the sense of delight that pervaded other work at this time.

Second Half of the Seventeenth Century

From scorching Spaine, and freezing Muscovie,
From fertill France, and pleasant Italy,
From Poland, Sweden, Denmarke, Germany,
And some of these rare Patterns have been set
Beyond the bounds of faithless Mahomet:
From spacious China, and those Kingdomęs East,
And from great Mexico, the Indies West.
Thus are these workes, farre fetcht, and dearely bought,
And consequently, good for Ladies thought.

J. Taylor, *The needle's Excellency*, 1636.

Very gradually during the 17th century a new source of ideas made its impact upon embroidery design. Merchants returning from the Far East, members of the East India Company brought with them for their families elaborately printed floral

(*Continued on page 76*)

---

49 (1), (2) *Embroideries from Hardwick Hall (cf.* (1) *with Fig.* 9, (1))
(3) *Detail from an unfinished late 16th-century cushion cover worked in coloured silk and gold thread on linen. Part is in plaited braid stitch, very fine tent stitch, and laid-work. The pattern is drawn in pale black. The outline of the diaper is worked in pale green in one place and gold thread in another*
(4A), (4B) *Detail and plan of an early 17th-century cushion, 17″ × 21″, worked in long and short and satin stitch in coloured silks, with laid and couched work, metal thread and spangles, on satin*
(5) *Pomegranate motif. Late 16th-century cushion*

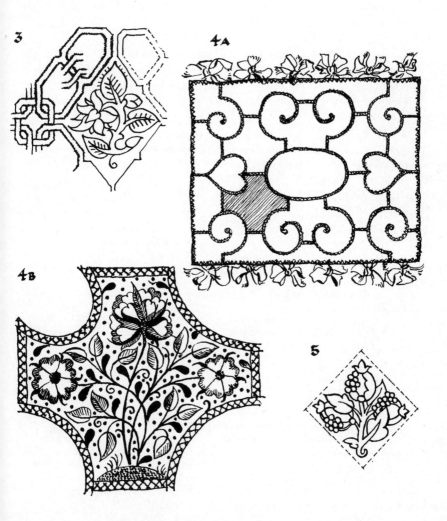

counterpanes which found their way into homes all over England. The colour range was limited, but the wide border designs and complicated tree or floral medallion patterns which covered the centre were rich in their variation and detail. Small wonder that such a gift should excite the women at home and act as a spur to their creative efforts. Soon curtains, bedspreads and bed-hangings were being embroidered with designs conceived on a much larger scale than hitherto. Linen evidently seemed too fine a fabric, cotton was not yet spun strongly enough to be used alone; the alternative, a linen warp with cotton weft, twill weave, proved admirable for the crewel wool embroidery worked upon it(50). "Crewel work" would be a more accurate name for this style than "Jacobean", by which it is generally known, for a similar use of wool appears in the Tudor period and may have developed from non-ecclesiatical mediaeval work. It lapsed in favour in the late 16th century until it was revived in the time of Queen Anne with a lighter approach to the tree motif. The term is scarcely applicable to the work of James I's reign which is still Elizabethan in character.

Unfortunately in the 20th century the so-called "Jacobean" design has been forced upon us in so mutilated a form, using such garish colours, whether reproduced on printed upholstery fabric or in stencilled embroidery designs that we have a completely false impression of the original style. In the 17th century, though the inspiration at first came from one source, India, results were most varied and arose from the needlewoman's command of a fair

(*Continued on page 78*)

---

50   *Motifs from crewel work curtains.* (1), (2) *and* (7) *show the full flowing line and turn-over, and the contrast between fern sprays and heavy fillings* (*seven different ones are not uncommon*)

    (1) *Second half 17th century, bed curtain in shades of indigo, dark blue, emerald green*

    (2) *Mid 17th-century curtain, leaf 18″, in shades of dark blue*

    (3) *Late 17th-century bed curtain, polychrome*

    (4) *Late 17th-century Indian bedspread worked in stem stitch*

    (5) *Mid 17th-century bed curtain, in shades of pink, outlined in heavy twisted cotton*

    (6) *Mid 17th-century bed curtain in shades of green; Singalese chain is used on outer tulip petals*

    (7) *Mid 17th-century bed curtains in shades of dark blue-green*

    (8) *Early 18th-century bed curtain*

    (9), (10) *From Abigail Pett's bed curtains*

    Drawings are not to the same scale

range of stitches which she used to create many different textures within a design bound together by a very limited colour scheme. It is true that the colours were then harder and brighter than we see them today, mellowed by three hundred years' exposure to daylight, but the vegetable dyes[1] then in use seldom, if ever, produced a colour that did not blend well, and the "Jacobean" needlewoman was possessed of a very sound judgement of tone values. She also retained the Elizabethan's robust imagination and fantasy, as anyone may see who will devote time to study the hangings on Abigail Pett's bed in the Victoria and Albert Museum.

In addition to ideas from foreign sources, designs were published in London towards the end of the 17th century. They may have been influenced by an earlier tradition because they show "slips" of fruit and flowers, and "details of birds on sprigs"—a beautifully drawn turkey is perched incongruously upon a small berried twig—in a manner which changed remarkably little for about a hundred years, from the middle of Elizabeth I's reign to 1667–1707 when John Overton and Peter Stent, publisher and engraver respectively, were at work.

THE HOME
Bed-furnishings

Some embroidery immediately arouses our curiosity about the people who made and used it. Was Abigail Pett a relative of Phineas Pett who wears the handsome embroidered cap in his portrait? Did she find the lion and camel in a pattern book and draw the squirrel from one on her own nut tree even though the tree grows on Chinese land? Would she, and her maids, gather dyestuffs for her wools and did they together decide that no two motifs should in colour be exactly alike? We can so easily imagine them sitting around these curtains, chattering away while their deft fingers chose wools from 13 different hanks to use in a quite limited number of stitches but

[1] *Vegetable dyes:*

Lemon-yellow	— Onion skins boiled in Brass kettle.
Golden yellow	— Onion skins boiled in Iron kettle.
Yellow-green	— St. John's wort and alum.
Vermilion-red	— Madder, alum, bran.
Magenta-purple	— Cochineal and alum.
Deep blue	— Indigo.
Deep black-purple	— Logwood and alum.
Blue-black	— Logwood and potash.

Various lichens—yellow—rust—according to where gathered. And many others.

51 *Details from Abigail Pett's bed.* A–D, *are from another 17th-century hanging*

with such versatility that the limitation is far from obvious (51).

A very different approach to design was shown a few years later by Mary Thurston and her sister Sarah, who in 1694 made the twin coverlets now in the Fitzwilliam Museum, Cambridge, and the Victoria and Albert Museum. These show all the delicacy of the early years of chinoiserie, in the openly spaced motifs, feathery leaves, phoenixes, peacocks, pagodas and palms, carnations, slender tulips and fanciful flowers worked in coloured silks and silver thread on white satin. No two motifs in the design are exactly alike, and there is no repeat in the border which, though the motifs are more closely arranged than in the centre of the bedspread, remains light. Each bedspread, 8′ ×7′ 3″, is worked in coloured silks with some metal thread on white satin. Mary's is signed and dated, and Sarah's bears her coat of arms.

An unquilted bedspread of humbler material, cloth, in dark brown, a colour so much used for a background in Scandinavian embroidery and tapestry weaving, is no less beautiful. Upon such a deep tone a good range of bright yellow-greens, pinks and some

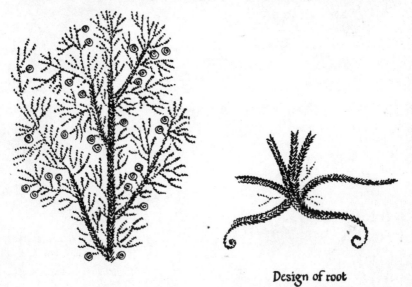

Design of root

52   *Top third of one repeat on a late 17th century bed curtain; worked in crewel wools in asparagus pattern, in greenish blue, with carmine berries. Stitches: coral knot, stem, herringbone and raised plaited knots*

Dragon, from Abigail Pett's bed hangings. Victoria and Albert Museum. Crown Copyright

Westminster Hospital Chapel altar frontal, designed and worked by Beryl Dean. Patchwork in many different fabrics, some embroidered in coloured metallic thread. Courtesy of the Chaplain, Westminster Hospital.

53   *Pillow cover*

soft blue has been used with richness in a floral design arranged in
six squares. Five contain a garland surrounding a conventionalised
flower; the sixth has a coat of arms; a vase of flowers fills the remaining space in the corner of each square; there is a slightly
wider border on each side than at the ends.

By the turn of the century the quilted style which became so
popular in the 18th century was established. A coverlet of outstanding beauty was made about 1700, entirely in shades of brown
and gold silk, worked in split, satin, and long and short stitch, with
various fillings of French knots and laid and couched work. It has
a trellis quilting in yellow silk back stitch. There are three graduated pillows to match, each carefully designed as a unit; these and
the quilt have a simple guilloche border about 1″ wide(53).

Designs on many contemporary bed hangings were quite large.
Leaves can be as long as 18″. Work of this size is invariably in
monochrome, often in shades of a rich indigo blue and is entirely of
swirling leaves, closely placed, leaving little background, and giving
scope for many surface fillings. Between these two extremes of
scale are the hangings worked in polychrome, usually with a dominant colour, with flowing stems or a Persian "Tree of Life" rising
from a ground of grass-grown mole hills each bearing a delicate
sprig, and probably somewhere in their midst a Chinese pagoda
and a Persian stag pursued by a leopard. Heavy foliage on the
main field of such curtains is contrasted with interspersed light
foliage; occasional phoenix-like birds with the pagoda proclaim

one of the countries of influence. China had yet to take complete hold of the embroideress' imagination for it was not until the later years of the century that Oriental objects were imported in sufficient quantity to affect style.

Three other types of design were also used on hangings. One is known as the asparagus pattern, the second is based on open scrolling stems and tendrils, and the third, less usual and more formal, is derived from woven fabrics.

Wall-hangings

Embroidered wall-hangings were still in use in the late 17th century but were soon to be superseded by paper painted in the Chinese manner. To the new fashion we owe the survival of the hangings found behind several layers of paper in a house in Hatton Garden, London, the canvas having been used as a support; rescued and cleaned, they are now in the Victoria and Albert Museum. They were probably made during the early years of Charles II's reign and consist of six panels, about 7′ 6″ × 3′ 10″, worked in coloured wools on canvas. The design shows a classical arcade with large unrelated twining leaves and flowers. Fruit hangs over each arch and there are birds at the top and animals at the foot of each column(54). Stitches used include tent, brick, rococo, cross and crosslet, with French knots and couched work. Rococo stitch is particularly effective and there are several interesting fillings which warrant close examination.

/ A completely different conception of wall decoration can be seen in a reception room in Penshurst Place, Kent, which was redecorated in the reign of William and Mary. The panelling was designed in the rococo style worked with applied brocade, the different colours held down with cord and $\frac{1}{2}$″ braid (55). A set of six chairs, two arm-chairs and one sofa were upholstered to match./

A group of pictorial hangings made for Stoke Edith, a house destroyed by fire in 1927, is now at Montacute House, Somerset. These are in tent stitch on canvas. One panel is copied from an engraving in Ogilby's *Virgil* (1658); the colour and stitchery have added much to the original. "The Orangery Garden", its companion, is drawn in perspective and has rather surprising cast shadows, some in dark brown, others in deep blue; equally unusual are orange trees growing in large Chinese porcelain vases of fine

54 *Dragon from the Hatton Garden hangings (V. & A.). Its eye and legs are in tent stitch and body in cross stitch; dark background in tent stitch and ground in Hungarian point*

linen decorated with chain stitch applied to the canvas. The general colour scheme is restrained. The employment of resident professional embroiderers over many weeks must have made this an extremely costly piece of work.

Samplers

In the 17th century we have the first tangible evidence of the way in which embroidery was taught. Named and dated samplers show the order in which a child learned different methods, sometimes assisted by foreign pattern books, these exercises to be followed by an embroidered cabinet; afterwards she would be allowed to help in larger household schemes.

The earliest samplers were made in the 16th century but none are now in existence. The first of those extant belongs to the early years of the 17th century and are covered with scattered motifs, birds and geometric patterns, obviously test pieces, on loosely woven linen fabric. Popular designs were recorded and new ideas were

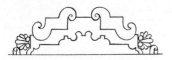

55 *Rococo motif similar to that used at Penshurst*

created in silk and metal thread, the whole specimen being added to as need arose. These early samplers show a diversity of ideas and methods which died out all too soon(56). One worked sometime between 1630 and 1660 resembles a cushion cover, with flowers and insects in coloured purl and red knots on white satin. A very fine sampler, $10\frac{1}{4}'' \times 21''$ (Met. Mus.), is worked in coloured silk and silver thread in tent, cross, rococo, Holbein, plaited braid, chain, Gobelin, and eyelet stitches; at the top are fruit and flower "slips", birds, insects and a boar, while about 36 geometric patterns, based generally upon the diamond, occupy the lower two thirds. Other samplers can be found in which rococo stitch or metal threads predominate; one of the latter shows 23 ways of using gold thread as a grounding and for lines and borders.

The sampler's wealth of information was worthy of a better arrangement, so it grew into a rather special piece of work of carefully considered design, often of great technical virtuosity, to be made by children between the age of seven and eleven as they learnt the craft.

One little girl, Martha Edlin, born in 1660, worked her coloured sampler in 1668, her white work sampler in 1669, finished a stump work box and needlework accessories in 1671 and her bead trinket box in 1673, which industry puts us to shame. Martha's first sampler is longer and narrower than her mother's would have been. It is on unbleached yellowish soft linen, about $8'' \times 30''$, worked in coloured silks. There are three alphabets in eyelet stitch, counted satin stitch and cross stitch, 12 or more bands of pattern

(*Continued on page 86*)

---

56   *Details from samplers.*

(1) *Silk on linen; cross, long-armed cross, double running and stem; third quarter 17th century*

(2) *Rococo, back stitch and spider webs; early 18th century*

(3) *Silk on linen; double running; one of eight different motifs in a band; sampler dated 1661*

(4) *White work sampler; linen on linen; part of an alphabet in buttonhole stitch and drawn thread work; 17th century*

(5) *Eyelet holes in two shades of green silk and interlaced knots in silver-gilt thread; late 17th century*

(6) *Diaper patterns in darning; one is worked in two directions; silk; last quarter 18th century*

(7) *All-over pattern of squares outlined in Roman stitch and filled alternately with rococo and two-sided Italian cross stitch; worked in pink and pea-green silk; 17th century*

(8) *All-over pattern of squares outlined in Roman stitch filled with rococo stitch worked diagonally in silk; plaited knots in metal thread; 17th century*

(9) *All-over pattern in rococo, plaited braid stitch and plaited knots; 17th century*

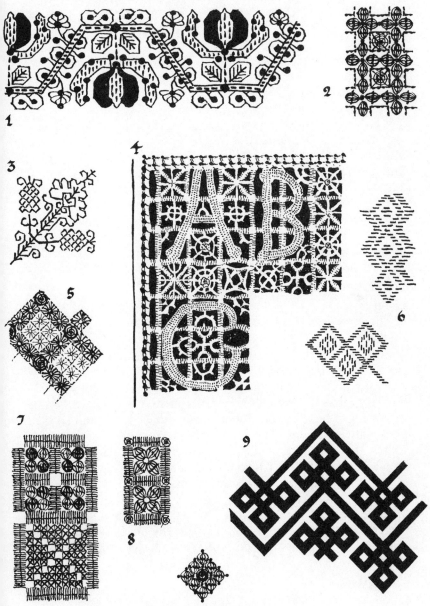

in a variety of stitches; it is signed and dated. Her white work sampler, about $8'' \times 13''$, has patterned bands set in yellowish linen. The tiny things she made include two pincushions in cross stitch and Florentine stitch, needle and bodkin cases, a miniature toy bellows similar to perfume bellows, $2''$ long gloves and a toy goose in silver thread. (See *Oxford Junior Encyclopedia*, Vol. XI, p. 305 for a coloured reproduction.)

White work samplers were detailed, very beautiful and of a very high technical standard. There are several in the Fitzwilliam Museum in Cambridge, and others in the Victoria and Albert Museum and private collections. They reflect the contemporary interest in Italian reticella lace which is largely based upon infinitesimal detached buttonhole stitches. A diversity of patterns was created upon white linen using white thread. Counted satin stitch borders and alphabets alternate with needlepoint in some samplers, while others are of successive bands of openwork.

A needlepoint sampler, $37\frac{1}{2}'' \times 5\frac{3}{4}''$, in the London Museum, has 15 bands of various widths.

Cabinets

In the 17th century small table cabinets became popular: the credit for one of these must be shared between the child embroideress and the cabinet maker, who from the collection of pieces sent to him devised in each case a unique object to be used for toilet articles, writing materials, or as a workbox. The embroidery might be partially or wholly in stump work, tent stitch with biblical pictures, bead work or in rather long satin stitches upon white satin with medallion portraits of Charles I and Henrietta Maria. If the cabinet were to be used as a needlework box many accessories would be made and decorated; cases for needles, scissors, inch-tape, thimble and a pincushion. Invariably, on lifting the lid a model garden appeared; the front doors when opened, revealed many small drawers to delight the young owner(57, $_4$). There are many cabinets still in existence, but as might be expected the standard of workmanship varies considerably.

Stump Work

Stump work originally was known as "raised work", its present name probably not being used before 1894. Of all the late

57 (1) *Tortoiseshell-framed toilet mirror (Met. Mus.). Stump work. White satin ground worked in coloured silk and purl, chiefly in needlepoint fillings, detached or padded; also long and short stitch and French knots. Dated 1672*
(2) *From a stump work picture (V. & A.) 17th century. Man worked in needlepoint fillings; pearl set in shoulder bow; hands wire; head, stockings and sleeves padded; dress, cloak and stocking turnovers hang free; ground of unravelled silk loops*
(3) *Stump work stag, heavily padded*
(4) *Writing and toilet cabinet (Met. Mus.) 17th century; chiefly laid silk on linen canvas*
(5) *Various uses of metal thread found in a stump work picture*

17th-century developments in design these embroidered fantasies are easily the most curious. The origin of raised embroidery can be traced back many years in both secular and ecclesiastical work and the use of high relief is not confined to England. It was but a short step from Elizabethan raised stems and detached buttonhole flowers to padded acorns covered with buttonhole stitch and roses with many separate freely standing petals, again in buttonhole stitch. Ingenuity led to the use of carved wooden moulds or wax for heads and hands, horsehair for stuffing bodies, held in place by crossed threads until covered with needlepoint, and glued canvas for canopies projecting beyond the figure being sheltered: all these things, scattered rather than designed, were used upon mirror frames, cabinets and pictures(57). The horror of an empty space is still apparent. Subjects are classical and biblical, drawn in outline upon the linen or silk fabric. The drawing is sometimes tinted as a guide and the colour is not always covered. Fine cord, gimp, seed pearls, spangles, pieces of coral and peacock feather can be found. In earlier work spangles cover the background but their use gradually died out. The last specimen of stump work is thought to have been completed about 1677. Stump work is as unpractical as any embroidery can be; it is a perfect dust collector and harbour for moth; that the examples we have are in such excellent condition indicates that in their own time they were greatly cherished and often kept under glass. If this work can be regarded with some tolerance, we shall find in it much amusing detail.

Needlework Pictures

Needlework pictures which developed in the Stuart period were created in petit point (tent stitch); stump work; bead work; or in loosely made long and short stitches on silk or satin, with spangles. There was sometimes a mediaeval tendency to split the design into bands. The subject matter ranged from the biblical and classical choice of the early 17th century to portraiture, and by the end of the century to flagrant imitation of engravings and paintings.

Upholstery

The stitches used on late 17th-century chairs were more varied than in the succeeding century. Turkey work regained favour. It is pleasantly warm to touch but this may not have been the reason for its use, rather an interest in texture is indicated on a chair which has a covering of black silk with the pattern only in the pile of Turkey work.

A chair of 1675, with a dark background to a floral design is worked in deep rich colours in tent, long and short, split, satin and Hungarian stitch. Others of 1690 and 1700 have classical subjects influenced by engravings, worked in tent stitch, and pastoral subjects were already being designed in the manner of the 18th century. This is in fact a period of transition where no clear line of demarcation can be made between the two centuries.

CLOTHES

An era of extravagance in clothing followed the drab years of the Commonwealth(58). The beauty of elaborate laces was enhanced

58 *Part of a blue satin petticoat (last quarter 17th century, 3′ 3″ × 8′ 9″) worked with silver-gilt and silver thread. The triple scroll continues across the whole width, but the sprigs only extend over the centre 4′, to the placket holes*

by the background of rich silks and satins which have not lasted over the years and once again we have to rely on portraits to implement our knowledge. Gold and silver lace, braids and ribbons appear at this time to have played a far more important part than embroidery in costume decoration.

Baby clothes, produced in quantity, are notable for their simplicity (60). The customary high standard for white work is

59   *Herald's Tabard (second half 17th century) such as would have been made in the workshops of Edmund Harrison, a member of the London Broderers' Company, from the reign of James I to Charles II. Worked in gold and coloured silk, with sequins, on velvet. Heavily embossed*

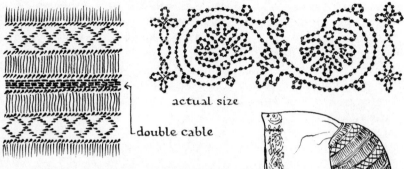

actual size

double cable

60   *Smocking on a 17th-century short bonnet (V. & A.) worked in white linen thread on linen; the edge has a scrolling design in coral stitch*

maintained. To this period belong the earliest extant examples of smocking, small areas set in bonnet crowns, apparently for decoration only, since the stitchery is too tight and the areas too small to allow any play of fabric(60). French knots appear to have been very popular indeed and are used with effect; they are small and tightly worked, essential on garments to be frequently laundered.

The Eighteenth Century

THE HOME

By the 18th century trade had extended beyond India to China. It is not easy for us to recreate the feeling of excitement which was caused by the first influx of Chinese works of art, though at all times to the Western eye the minute detail of much Eastern craftsmanship will always be impressive. Certainly the impact on the early 18th century was most forceful, and "chinoiserie", the vogue for things Chinese, invaded the English

home. Embroidery followed the fashionable trend in design shown
in furniture and silver, to name only two of the many crafts
affected. The mixture of Chinese and Indian influence which could
be seen in late 17th-century embroidered bed hangings, in the
conventionalised hummocks of ground from which the tree patterns
spring, gradually gave way to a completely Chinese domination.
We have seen that delicate work existed at the same time as the
heavy crewel-work curtains, yet it may be that the preponderance
of these served to emphasise the delicacy of Chinese silk, the very
small silk stitchery, chiefly chain, upon it, and the light airiness of
their bird and flower motifs(61).

Delicacy is not a characteristic of the whole century, however.
Had the 18th-century houses been less perfectly proportioned,
with rooms less lofty and spacious, the orgy of flowers indulged in
from the time of the later Stuarts, William and Mary, and Queen
Anne, to the mid 18th century, would have been completely over-
whelming. Floral designs on clothing were echoed in floral chairs,
settees and stools, in pole screens, in embroidered carpets and
hangings, and in bed-furnishings. Nor were the flowers always
derived from the more refined Indian and Chinese elements, more
often they were inspired by the peony with large waving petals.
This exotic style with very robust drawing and colour was conveyed
to the English garden flowers with which Oriental species combined so well. Often naturalism was the aim, not always achieved;
sometimes the designer would choose shells, ribbons and festoons
in the rococo style, combined with Chinese frets and phoenixes;
occasionally every square inch of fabric was covered. Professional
designers worked also from collections of flower prints, while great
Dutch flower paintings of the 17th century must have been an

(Continued on page 94)

---

61   *Details of Chinoiserie designs and quilting patterns.*
     *(1), (4), (5), (6) From a coverlet (Met. Mus.). Linen ground, with chinoiserie
     designs in coloured silk in chain, stem, buttonhole and other stitches. The
     quilting is in cream-coloured silk in back stitch. Late 17th century to early
     18th century*
     (2) Gold thread couched with silk to form quilting
     *(3) Curtain (V. & A.) worked in long and short and satin stitch in silk on
     linen. Early 18th century*
     *(7), (8) Typical background patterns for quilting in running or back stitch.
     (7) is often used for false quilting which is through two thicknesses of linen
     without padding*

additional source of inspiration. Yet in spite of this plethora of foliage, good taste somehow prevailed. Professor Trevelyan gives a wonderful picture of the 18th century at its best:

> If the England of the 18th century, under aristocratic leadership, was a land of art and elegance, its social and economic structure was assistant thereto. As yet there was no great development of factories, producing goods wholesale, ruining craftsmanship and taste, and rigidly dividing employers from employed. A large proportion of wage-earners were fine handicraftsmen, often as well educated, as well-to-do and socially as well considered as the small employer and shopkeeper.
>
> Under these happy conditions, the skilled hands produced, for the ordinary market, goods of such beautiful design and execution that they are valued by connoisseurs and collectors today: china, glass and other ware, silver plate, books beautifully printed and bound, Chippendale chairs and cabinets, all sorts of articles for ornament and use. Even the commonest type of grandfather-clocks that told the time in farmhouse kitchens, were simple and decorative in design, the outcome of a tradition followed with individual variations by innumerable small firms.[1]

Upholstery

There is in Temple Newsam House, Leeds, a great suite of 20 carved gilded chairs, four settees and a day bed worked in wool and silk. It was commissioned between 1738–47. The colour is startling, a mustard yellow background with a design of bright flowers wholly in red, blue and white with greenish foliage. Such a set would normally have 12 or 13 chairs and might be professionally made, but in the majority of cases where fewer pieces were needed the embroidery was done at home. Technically the work was often uneven, suggesting that more than one person contributed her share to each piece. Cross stitches, where used, do not all cross in the same direction, though where this is done deliberately to give variety in texture, the intention is obvious.

Irregularities also occur in tent stitch. Silk was commonly used for detail to give further variation, the stitches being made quarter size by splitting the number of threads used for the other work. In small upright chairs both seat and back are worked, the embroidery being shaped to the wooden frame; in winged arm-chairs,

[1] *History of England*, Chap. XIII.

seat, back and arms are completely covered with embroidered upholstery (62).

In design the background is always floral and some chairs are entirely so; others have a background of two colours separated by a band of strapwork and rococo shells. Many have, within a similar frame, a pastoral scene or fable, often copied from a painting or book-illustration. Others depict incidents in family history or bear a coat of arms. The colour as it is now, rich and comfortable from years of exposure to light and use, gives little indication of the

62   Wing chair (*Met. Mus.*). *On canvas in wool and silk entirely in tent stitch. Natural colours on light brown. 1725*

original fierce brilliance; that so many chairs have survived speaks highly of the durability of tent stitch and the quality of the wool that was used. However, the fashion for striped Spitalfields silk in upholstery design must have come none too soon for those of discernment and in the second half of the century silk or tapestry was preferred.

Turkey work persisted; a large number of chairs in this method was ordered for the Houses of Parliament in 1739.

Carpets

Critics such as Addison in *The Spectator* complained that too much time and money was spent embellishing the home, but the professional embroiderers reaped a harvest during this period, for they must have been responsible for a large proportion of the work.

Large embroidered carpets were unlikely to be attempted at home; the task of drawing the design alone was beyond any but the skilled professional. Early Georgian carpets have endured well. They were worked in wool with a little silk, chiefly in cross stitch on coarse canvas. The strongly constructed designs have a tumultuous array of huge flowers and ribbons in brilliant colours against a darker background, and may well have been very disturbing when seen beneath large sets of embroidered chairs also flower-smothered, in equally bright colours. The designs themselves were excellent, being very closely knit. There is usually a wide flowing border around a central bouquet which spreads without repetition into the four corners. Compared with such profusion the Elizabethan floral world was selective and restrained.

Wall-hangings

Very few wall-hangings were worked in the 18th century. Those at Wallington Hall, finished in 1716, and a set at Newliston, near Edinburgh, are still in the homes for which they were intended, while the Ashton Hall set, dated 1744 and signed Mary Holt, is now in the Birmingham City Art Gallery. Those at Wallington

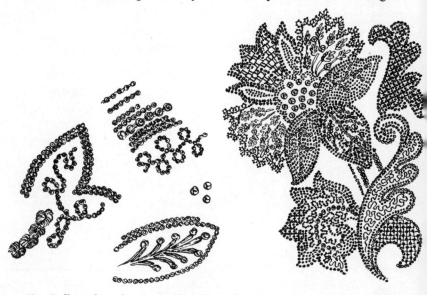

63   *Coffee-coloured string on dark brown linen; second quarter 18th century*

▲ *Part of a bed valance, late 16th century. Cynaras and Myrrha; linen canvas worked with coloured wools and silks in tent stitch and raised work. Victoria and Albert Museum, Crown Copyright*

Woman's hood, late 16th century. Black silk on linen, worked in stem and double
▼ *coral stitches, and speckling. Victoria and Albert Museum, Crown Copyright*

▲ *Embroidered pillow cover, late 16th century. White satin ground with canvas appliqué worked in silver thread and coloured silks. Victoria and Albert Museum, Crown Copyright*

Upholstered chair, abo 1685, from Drayton Hous Northamptonshire. Canv embroidered with colour wools and silks in ten Hungarian, long and sho split and satin stitches. V toria and Albert Museu Crown Copyright

Hall are in tent stitch in wool on fine canvas and represent either garden or country scenes with fashionable people at their leisure pursuits. The Newliston wall decorations consist of twelve large embroideries set into Adam panelling. They are on cream watered silk, in wool appliqué, with detail partly in silk and partly water-colour. The designs are in keeping with the Adam style, using acanthus scrolls, urns and sphinxes.

A curious feature of this period was the "string knotting" craze amongst fashionable women headed by royalty(63). It was an odd form of recreation, but a glance at the hanging made by Princess Amelia, as excellent a design as many contemporary carpets and not dissimilar, shows much ingenuity in the use of varied thicknesses of string and disposition of knots couched down to form a resultant texture and pattern that is wholly admirable.

Bed-furnishings

Though some bed-furnishings continued to be made in the 18th century, interest formerly shown in bed valances and curtains was transferred to the coverlet with its accompanying set of three matching graduated pillows and bolster for daytime use. There are sets of these in museums and private collections, all too even in technical quality to be the work of amateurs. Their beauty can only be fully appreciated when it is actually seen, for they lose much in reproduction. All are quilted and worked in

64 *Embroidered satin coverlet for the State bed at Osterley; designed by Robert Adam, 1776*

silk, and from 1714–60 were more often upon a silk than a linen ground. Handsome designs are based upon a wide range of English, Oriental and highly conventionalised flowers, the rococo C curl and shell motif. Back stitch, generally in yellow silk but occasionally in red or green, is used more often than running stitch for the quilting itself, to form a texture against which the motifs, worked in a wide range of coloured silks, are evenly distributed.

Corded quilting in white linen thread on cotton was used for both pillow and cot covers in the first half of the 18th century (V. & A.), while the end of the century saw the rise in popularity in humbler homes of the patchwork quilt upon one version of which appliqué designs were made with floral motifs cut from printed cottons, and stitched on to a cotton ground.

During the late Georgian period embroidery is less prominent because it failed to harmonise with the lighter style of furniture. The State bed hangings at Osterley are an exception (64).

Small Pieces of Furniture

On small objects tapestry was used as often as embroidery. The subject matter was similar and at a distance it is difficult to distinguish between them. Pole screens were not unconnected with vanity. Created in the 18th century to protect the make-up worn by elegant women from the heat of large open fires, they were very practical little pieces of furniture, being rectangular, oval, square or shield shaped, upon a turned pole, so that they could be raised and lowered at will (65). Pastoral subjects were usually in tent stitch in silk upon fine canvas; designs of flowers, bouquets, ferns, ribbons and tassels springing from an urn (Etruscan revival) were either in varied silk stitchery on satin, or in tent stitch on canvas if enclosed in a rococo border. The designs always showed more restraint than

65 *Panel for a pole screen* (*Met. Mus.*). *Tent stitch on canvas worked in coloured wool. The design shows a shepherdess in a pastoral setting. Size 9″ × 11¾″. Early 18th century*

other contemporary work, and by comparison even appear uninspired. Fire fans, first known about 1690, were used for the same purpose. Card tables too were embroidered. In one made by Adam, at Penshurst Place, Kent, a pastoral design worked in fine tent stitch covers the gaming surface and is protected by glass.

Samplers

The 18th-century sampler is a framed decoration calling for only a modicum of the skill required of the 17th-century child. Inspiration which produced the muslin apron sampler mentioned again under "Aprons in the 18th Century" (p. 108), and a very fine darning sampler (V. & A.) was indeed rare. It was hoped that a little geography would be inculcated into the minds of any young ladies who worked, monotonously in coloured outlines, the counties of England and countries of Europe on map samplers. The most popular style during the second half of the 18th and early 19th centuries was a cross stitch record of a house, symbolic garden, ABC, text or poem and a border. Those of the 18th century often have a row of coronets, each with an initial beneath, to denote king, duke, marquis, and other ranks of the nobility.[1]

It is refreshing to find an individual sampler of 1761 worked by E. Philips, aged seven, which shows her house standing in a clearing in a pine wood indicated by rows of conventionalised trees. Her father, mother and five sisters, the youngest with her nurse, and one brother with his tutor are nearby, and the servants, one of whom is a coloured woman, and one a little black boy. Probably her father travelled, because the ocean, a ship, a crocodile, black swans and other birds appear. Beneath is a monogram, G.R.III, supported by soldiers in contemporary costume, and in the lowest band, the name and date and a border of flowers. The colour scheme is mainly in shades of blue and green. It is a naïve, very attractive piece of work.

CLOTHES

The opulence in household furnishings is in contrast to the embroidery on clothes, which, though rich, was always well-placed, usually restrained and often very delicate in colour; it too was predominantly floral, as if joyously escaping from Commonwealth austerity and the vogue for plain satin which immediately followed.

[1] M. Huish, *Samplers and Tapestry Embroideries*, 1913. Plate IX.

A flourishing silk industry had developed at Spitalfields, specialising in delicate woven stripe and sprig designs which were complete in themselves yet at the same time an excellent background for embroidery in silk. By the mid-18th century London was the clearing house for Far Eastern trade. Cotton goods came in quantity from India, fine Madras muslin being particularly in demand. A cotton weaving industry developed in this country to help satisfy current needs, which were considerable for clothing by the end of the 18th and in the early 19th century.

Portraits of fashionable men and women give the general effect of clothes that were worn, but painting, having at last developed greater freedom and lost the detailed style shared by the Elizabethan miniaturist, cannot henceforth be relied upon to give accurate information about threads and stitches; it is fortunate that so many whole and fragmentary garments still exist.

MEN'S CLOTHES—WAISTCOATS AND COATS

The 18th-century gentleman was the last of many generations to hang embroidered clothes of any note in his closet, and although he might own a printed linen quilted morning-gown (1770; London Museum), of all his apparel, only coat and waistcoat were decorated. There are two styles of waistcoat, one sleeveless to be worn beneath a coat(66, $_1$), and the other with sleeves, a more handsome garment to be worn indoors after the outer coat had been removed(66, $_2$). In both the decoration consists of a strong border design from neck to hem on either side of the front opening, usually continued round the skirt, with additional emphasis on pocket flaps and cuffs. The rest of the fabric is often further embellished with a light sprig pattern. Buttons are always embroidered.

(Continued on page 102)

---

66 (1) *Sleeveless waistcoat. Coloured silks on a light ground*
(2) *Waistcoat of linen with false quilting in yellow silk; the floral ornament is worked in coloured silk twist in encroaching satin stitch with stems and centres in couched gold thread. Quilting pattern indicated on sleeve. Drawn to a smaller scale than (3)*
(3) *Flat strips of gold laid over thin card and caught down with closed herringbone*
(4) *Design from the front of a plum-coloured silk waistcoat, worked mainly in white with a little blue and the leaves in shaded green silk*
(5) *Early 18th-century man's cap in coloured silks on linen*

The Metropolitan Museum has a very fine sleeved waistcoat of linen with false quilting in yellow silk heavily enriched with floral ornament worked in coloured silks in long and short stitch, with stems and flower centres in silver-gilt thread. A wide border runs from high neckline to hem and continues around the fairly full skirt. Sleeves are embroidered from tight wrist to elbow and large low-set pocket flaps repeat the border motifs. Scattered at intervals are highly conventionalised fruits. There are 38 embroidered buttons and buttonholes down the 41″ of its total length(66, $_2$).

Another sleeved waistcoat (V. & A.) is of yellow satin, embroidered in coloured silks and metal thread in long and short stitch and couched work. This is 40″ long and fuller in the skirt than the slightly earlier garment in the Metropolitan Museum. The sleeves are left plain, pocket flaps are shaped and set higher, within reach of the hand, and there are only 21 embroidered buttons. The ornament is swirling and vigorous; large peony-type flowers are dominated by feather motifs which take the place of leaves.

On the whole the design upon sleeveless waistcoats is lighter, with sprig and feather motifs, many showing strong Persian influence(66 $_1$, 67). One sleeveless waistcoat (V. & A.) is made of white silk and worked in coloured silks with metal thread, sequins and metal disks: the ground has a typical small sprig pattern and the border has flowers and various leaves alternating with long gold leaves.

(Continued on page 104)

---

67   (1), (4) *From waistcoats worked in coloured silks on a light ground; about 1770*
     (2) *18th-century buttons*
        A. *Spider web in overcast wire frame*
        B. *Brown silk flat stitch and overcast*
        C. *1″ diam. worked in white and two greens on purple silk, one of eleven down a coat front. Three on each cuff have a green silk ground*
        D. *Green silk button on waistcoat to match* (C)
        E, F. *Waistcoat buttons*
     (3) *Feather and flower details showing Persian influence, from waistcoats made 1750–1807 for Baron Stanley of Alderney (Whitworth Art Gallery, Manchester)*
     (5) *Detail from purple satin coat (Platt Hall, Manchester). In the green satin waistcoat the same design is repeated except that purple satin replaces green in the border and the small leaves are filled with purple where they fall against white or green. Buttons 2c and 2D belong to this set. 1770–85*

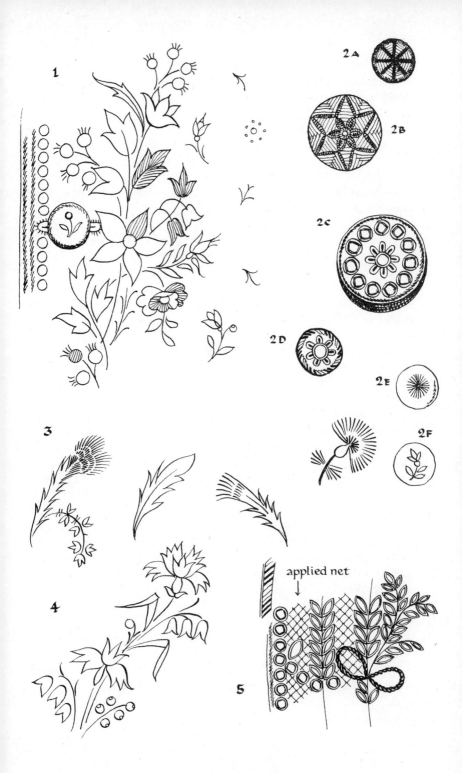

1

2A

2B

2C

2D

2E

2F

3

4

5

applied net

A man's court suit (dated 1785; in the London Museum) is made of brownish-black silk with a purple pin stripe which from a distance gives a rich iridescence. The coat is embroidered mainly in white, with a design of feathers and flowers; a little green is introduced in the leaves and a small amount of blue in the flowers. There are ten 1″ buttons down the front and three on each cuff.

Embroidered caps, worn indoors when the wig was removed, continued to be made and were ornamented with floral designs similar to those upon waistcoats (66, $_5$).

On men's clothes a comparatively small amount of metal thread is used. It can be found laid across thin card cut to a rococo design and secured with double back stitch; also very fine strips of "plate" occur in flower centres; other devices used with restraint which add variety to the silk, are applied net, gold tinsel, small pieces of mirror glass showing Indian influence; and there are small steel sequins.

WOMEN'S CLOTHES

Comparatively few 18th-century women's dresses have been stored away in family chests and attics. The silk or satin of which the majority were made was perishable and many of them were no doubt remodelled for children to wear, since their costume was a miniature of adult style.

The following notable dresses represent the contrasting Early and Late Georgian styles; the earlier example, in the Metropolitan Museum collection, made at the very end of the 17th or the beginning of the 18th century is of dark grey woollen fabric with narrow woven stripes alternately brown and blue, edged with red. The under skirt is embroidered all over with silver-gilt thread in a light rococo design reflecting French taste (68). The over dress and train have a matching border and the woven stripes are worked alternately with star-like motifs and a running leaf pattern. The later example, in the London Museum, is a woman's court dress (1780), with panniers and train, made of powder-blue satin embroidered with vertical wave lines and very dainty flowers, mainly in white silk with touches of pink, yellow and green. Variation is obtained from the use of floss silk and horsetail, a tightly twisted silk, and from flat stitchery contrasted with groups of circular flowers each outlined with raised satin stitch (71, $_2$). The

68 *Dress (Met. Mus.). Grey wool with brown and blue stripes which are indicated in the diagram. Embroidery is entirely in silver-gilt thread. The rococo C curl dominates the design. Late 17th or early 18th century*

skirt is festooned with applied lace, each loop caught with a bow of white spots edged with blue cord.

In a woman's costume, besides the main fabric of the dress, three parts were given special attention, the stomacher, apron and petticoat.

Stomachers

The detachable stomacher, V-shaped from square neck to its point slightly below the natural waistline, was tightly stretched

69 *Motif from an early 18th-century piece of white work, possibly the border to a cap; Italian quilting in linen thread; open work and French knots. Sometimes Italian quilting is simulated on muslin by means of padded double back stitch*

over a stiffened corset to show the embroidery to advantage. There were several different styles. One example in the Victoria and Albert Museum shows Italian quilting on linen with a background of open work (71, ₁). False quilting, worked through two thicknesses of fabric without padding, was also used (69). Others became very elaborate to compete with the rich brocades available; influenced by the French mode, embroidery was almost submerged beneath a welter of tinsel, jewels, pearls, sequins, gold and silver lace, ruching, tassels and raised work.

70   *17th-century apron*

Aprons

Embroidered aprons were made only for decoration. Their treatment was varied but the size was always about 36″ × 18″, whether the fabric was silk, taffeta, satin or muslin. Except in the case of muslin the colour was usually cream but sometimes green, lilac or a bright yellow were used. These were always worked in silk, rarely in one colour, in rather large stitchery using long and short,

(*Continued on page 108*)

71   (1) *Stomacher. White false quilting. 1690–1710*
       (2) *Part of a running border on the train of a blue satin dress. Spots are slightly raised applied white satin sewn down with blue overcasting. 18th century*
       (3) *A pair of quilted pockets with a floral border in coloured silks. 18th century*

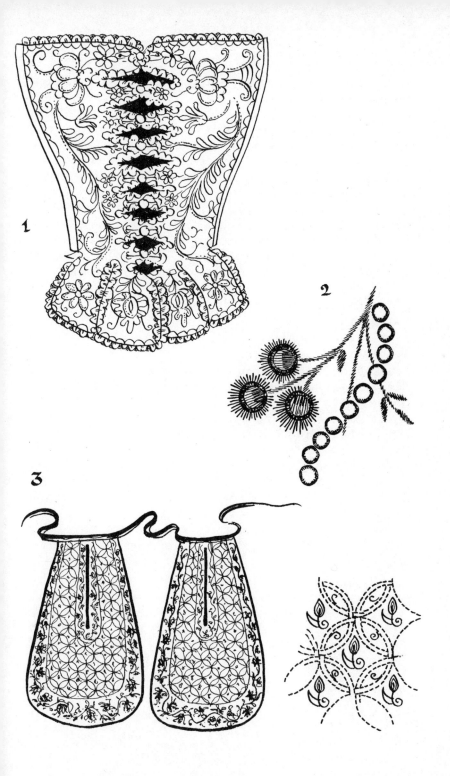

satin, stem, chain, French knots, couching, laid-work and other stitches, with silver, silver-gilt thread and sequins, metal strips and beads. Sometimes the design is entirely in chain stitch in the Far Eastern manner, sometimes in laid metal thread. Obviously they were not intended to be washed. The colours are inclined to be gaudy and the designs vary considerably, though flowers always predominate (70). These may spring from a cornucopia, or, coiling stems, or be arranged in a small spray accompanied by "chinoiserie" birds and rococo devices; they may have three large peony-type plants, or floral borders which either cover the whole fabric or travel down both sides and across the lower edge which is frequently shaped in several large scallops. There is one example of a muslin apron which was worked as a sampler, signed and dated 1709–18, with a great variety of pulled fabric stitches in a repeating pattern of attenuated trees with phoenixes and conventionalised flowers and leaves.

Petticoats

Petticoats became so elaborate and important an accessory that during their heyday vanity dictated the dress should be split in the front to expose the garment beneath.

Most petticoats were quilted and the best embroidery is of a very high standard. Much work is in very small back stitch, each stitch about one millimetre in size. Embroidery is in white or yellow silk and in addition to back, chain and running stitch there are other embellishments to the design in the form of silver, and silver-gilt thread and fine cord which we do not usually associate with quilting.

From the following quotation it is apparent that the petticoat could be the occasion of much rivalry (although those still preserved suggest more restraint in design than was in fact the case):

> Lady Huntingdon's petticoat was black velvet embroidered with chenille, the pattern a *large stone vase* filled with *ramping flowers* that spread almost over a breadth of the petticoat from the bottom to the top; between each vase of flowers was a pattern of gold shells and foliage embossed and most heavily gilt . . . it was a most laboured piece of finery, the pattern much properer for a stucco staircase than the apparel for a lady.[1]
>
> [1] Letter dated January 1738–39. "Mrs. Delany's Letters."

Women's Pockets

A woman's pockets were deeply hidden beneath her petticoat, which with the dress had slits in the side seams for access. They were two flat bags, somewhat pear-shaped, about 14″ long, sewn to a tape which tied round the waist. There was a vertical opening about 7″ long, with bound edges. Decoration was sometimes of tent stitch, Florentine and other canvas stitchery, or of a light scrolling floral design on linen, or of quilting in running or back stitch in simple geometric patterns (71, $_3$). False quilting, unpadded, was also used.

Accessories

Shoes were embroidered on canvas in Florentine and tent stitch, and on satin in coloured silk with floral designs. Linen corsets were quilted; straw "garden" hats also had their share of stitchery, as did dainty muslin handkerchiefs. Very fine white work on sheer Indian muslin, though fashionable during the last decade of the 18th century, developed to its fullest extent in the early 19th century.

The Nineteenth Century

The vast economic and social changes which took place during the 19th century had a far-reaching and serious effect upon the work of all craftsmen. We have seen that the products of the 18th century were sometimes ostentatious and that the quantity of embroidery produced was criticised for being excessive, but the individual quality of each piece of work was invariably good. During the 19th century the craftsman, faced for the first time with mechanisation and mass production, lost respect for his materials, deeming cleverness to be of greater importance than artistic integrity. Embroidery followed the common trend. Inventions directly affecting the craft include machines for quilting (1790), for tambour work[1] (1807), and for the manufacture of net (1809). In 1834 an embroidery machine was made on the Continent and in 1849 the sewing machine was patented in England.

[1] Tambour work gives the appearance of chain stitch. It is worked with a hook, from the back of fine material stretched in a round, or tambour, frame.

In spite of changing conditions and a new dilettante attitude, there were in isolated parts of the country several embroidery methods of considerable importance in use, white work in Ayrshire, quilting in Durham and Wales, and smocking, our nearest approach to a "peasant" craft, in all country districts.

WHITE WORK
The most beautiful embroidery of the 19th century was known as Ayrshire work, a name it did not receive until the late 1830's. It

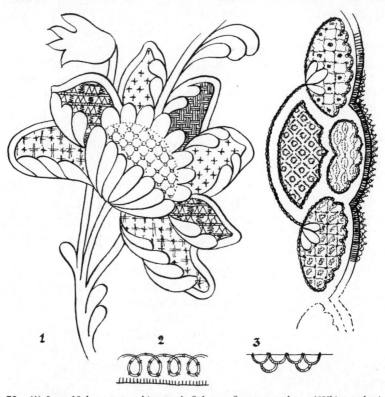

72   (1) *Late 18th-century white work fichu on fine cream lawn* (Whitworth Art Gallery, Manchester). *Corner and borders have a conventionalised flower and leaf design in a great variety of pulled fabric stitches and shadow work, the double back stitch giving a raised effect on the front. The buttonhole edging has delicate picots*
(2) *18th-century apron edge*
(3) *Edge to baby's cap. 1700–50*

originated in Dresden work: drawn fabric work used for men's shirt ruffles, brought to this country in 1782 by Luigi Ruffini who settled in Edinburgh, an arrival well timed to coincide with the sudden rise in popularity of cotton as a dress fabric. By the end of the 18th century cotton goods

> used by all classes in England, were already a formidable rival to "good English cloth". In a pamphlet of 1782 we read: "As for the ladies, they wear scarcely anything now but cotton, calicoes, muslin, or silks, and think no more of woollen shifts than we think of an old almanac. We have scarcely any woollen now about our beds but blankets, and they would most likely be thrown aside, could we keep our bodies warm without them."[1]

Yet in Scotland many young girls and women found employment in the new industry, which eventually shifted to the west as it became the centre of muslin manufacture.

The fine, soft, hand-woven muslin was transparent enough for a design drawn on card to show through, and to make work easier it was stretched over a hoop so that several children at a time could be occupied at the satin stitch dots before handing over to experienced women who worked the flower sprigs and borders. These were in chain stitch, a legacy from the East, darning stitch and drawn fabric stitches, with couching in a thicker thread to add variety and to increase the different tones of white.

The high standard of design introduced by Ruffini was continued by training in design for the muslin industry at the School of Design, Edinburgh. Fresh impetus came in 1814 as a result of bringing a French baby-robe embellished with needlepoint fillings to Scotland. Inspired by this, a woman designer-technician insisted on a more professional standard from her workers producing morning caps, cuffs, handkerchiefs, fichus, collars, tippets, pelerines, women's dresses, baby clothes and nightcaps.

In baby clothes both long and short dresses have a triangle of embroidery from skirt hem to bodice, with an inverted triangle on the bodice(73). Baby-caps and bonnets are usually of sheer linen cambric; the circular crown, made professionally, could be bought to be made up at home. Lace fillings soon supplanted drawn fabric work in popularity. White work reached its peak by 1857, though

[1] Trevelyan, *English Social History*.

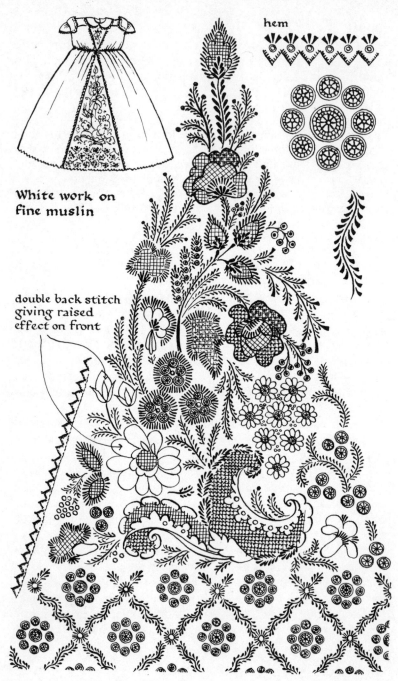

White work on
fine muslin

hem

double back stitch
giving raised
effect on front

73　*Baby's dress*

▲ *Part of a sampler signed and dated Elizabeth Mackett 1696. Complete sampler includes two more counted satin stitch borders and two of needlepoint lace fillings. Victoria and Albert Museum, Crown Copyright*

Cabinet, with miniature garden. Third quarter 17th century. Worked with silk, metal thread and purl, on satin. The side panel shows Eliezer and Rebekah; on the left door,
▼ *Abraham kneels before an angel. Victoria and Albert Museum, Crown Copyright*

▲ *Abigail Pett's bed curtains and valances, second half 17th century. Wool on cotton-linen twill weave. No two motifs are identical in stitch or colour. Victoria and Albert Museum, Crown Copyright*

some very good work was done until 1880. Its decline can be attributed to a change in dress fashions; about 1870 the bustle with its heavier fabrics ousted the crinoline; to the invention of the embroidery machine even earlier, about 1840, and to the increasing habit of buying material and even ready-made clothes in the shops.

There are two derivatives of Ayrshire work. In 1830 it was taken to Ireland where it became Mountmellick work, and about 1850 it reached Madeira; both styles developed individually.

QUILTING

Petticoats, warmly padded, continued to be worn in the 19th century but it is for their fine bed quilts worked to traditional patterns that Durham and Welsh quilters are justly famous.

Unlike 18th-century quilting, which was chiefly in back stitch, that of the 19th century is worked in running stitch; consequently it is not so detailed. A greater difference lies in the fact that it is rarely united with surface stitchery, while the bed quilts have the further distinction that one side has a patchwork design, the units not necessarily being related to the quilted pattern upon the reverse side of plain white linen.

English quilting patterns have richly flowing borders and a strong central design developed from a few shapes including the guilloche, rosette, feather and festoon repeated by means of templates. Essentially simple, they are in final effect elaborate and their technical perfection is of a high quality.[1]

SMOCKING

The 19th-century smock is the final development of a simple garment worn by the countryman from mediaeval times. Constructed from a series of rectangles of tough home-spun linen it was an admirable protection against weather in the days before rubber and plastics were known. Decorative stitchery had a two-fold purpose: where extra fullness was required it controlled the gathers, while on back and front panels and on collars and cuffs designs told the wearer's occupation. One colour only was used in patterns which gained their effect from changes in tone caused by the arrangement of various lines of stitches.

[1] See Barbara Snook, *Learning to Embroider* and A. Colby, *Patchwork*.

74   *Border of a white cotton dress (1815–20) worked in Broderie Anglaise*

BRODERIE ANGLAISE

Broderie Anglaise is a form of white work distinct from Ayrshire work. It is much simpler, based upon the repetition of many small holes, normally circular or oval in shape, with overcast edges and the design linked with similar areas of satin stitch and a little stem stitch.

Throughout the country many yards of Broderie Anglaise were embroidered for the "invisible" hems of petticoats, long drawers, chemises, nightdresses, camisoles, and sometimes emerged to decorate flounces on cotton day dresses (74). Many of the patterns

(*Continued on page 116*)

75   (1) *Early 19th-century shawl; 45½″ × 48½″; cream muslin worked on two diagonal corners on upper and lower side of material so that when folded for wear, both patterns are on the right side. Chain stitch in coarse thread gives the effect of applied braid; French knots and drawn fabric stitches are also used*
(2) *Muslin scarf (1835–6), in satin, stem and buttonhole stitch and openwork fillings*

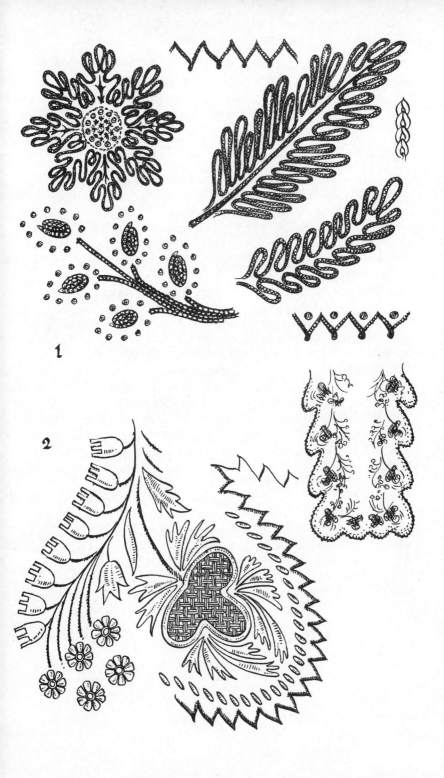

were from transfers, all the sewing was strong and capable of hard frequent laundering, and needles must have been plied with more energy than we are led to believe was possessed by elegant Victorian women.

BERLIN WOOLWORK

As we have seen, throughout its long history English embroidery has usually assimilated new ideas to advantage. This was not the case when Berlin woolwork was introduced from Germany and we cannot yet be said to have escaped entirely from its toils. The name is derived from the fact that both designs and wools came from Berlin. Soft canvas was painted in colour ready to work in cross stitch, in brilliant worsteds, aniline dyed, including vivid greens and magenta, intense purple, bright yellow, turquoise and various tone-discordant browns and beige. It was not until 1830 that any great quantity was imported and the craze which developed here was echoed in America by 1856. The subject matter of the pictures included pet dogs alone or with a little Victorian girl, a parrot on a wreath, lions, herds of deer—animals were given glass eyes to aid the naturalistic effect—and sprays of roses entwined with ivy.[1]

Ignoring the many generations of capable needlewomen behind her, the Victorian lady decided that her eyes were too weak for delicate embroidery. An American writer caustically comments, "lack of exercise would weaken any muscles—eyes included."[1] We cannot believe, however, that dim sight muted the colours of Berlin wool. It suddenly became genteel to embroider paper-weights, men's braces, slippers, lamp mats, chair backs, smoking caps, tobacco bags, screens, banners, carriage bags, hair tidies, pin-cushions, spectacle and comb cases and what-nots.[2]

It is to our shame that a hundred years later we are still able to buy painted canvas in reproduction of "Old Masters", with the only saving grace that the coloured wools provided are pre-selected with greater care.

---

[1] Harbeson.
[2] " 'what-not' . . . a very commodious little article which is meant to be suspended between windows or in any other convenient place." G. B. Harbeson, *American Needlework*, 1938.

76 *Victorian table centre. The design is machine printed on cream taffeta and worked in heavily twisted silk and narrow, shaded silk ribbon. This is part of a circular design with sprigs and festoons of roses and forget-me-nots. All flowers are of ribbon which is cleverly handled (Emb. Guild Coll.)*

OTHER NINETEENTH-CENTURY EMBROIDERY

Another whim, derived unwittingly from the 17th century, for beadwork upon mirror frames, tidies, garters, scent bottles, and candlesticks, kept the gentlewoman occupied; and other trivia which could not escape her needle included pen wipers, watch pads with a motto, and book markers with texts.

The motto, pious poem or text was the keynote of the Victorian sampler, which with almost unfailing regularity contained also the

77 *Victorian teapot stand, 1857, about 8″ square, in beadwork and cross stitch. A purple book and grey anchor lie within a pink and green rose wreath, all in wool, against a background of transparent glass beads surrounded by a narrow cross stitch border in two shades of pink and green wool; the sides are festooned with white opaque and transparent beads mounted over green felt (Emb. Guild Coll.)*

78 *Corner of a Victorian
bag on double thread canvas;
flowers, two tones of white
opaque glass beads, each with
a central pearl surrounded by
faceted gunmetal beads;
background of pink silk cross
stitch with the upper thread
in the reverse direction from
usual; edged with shaded
pink cord (Emb. Guild Coll.)*

façade of a house, supported by ornamental trees and flying birds,
one or more alphabets, a narrow border and the name and age of
the child with the year in which the work was finished. Any devia-
tion from cross stitch on fine woollen canvas (tammy) was rare.
Within these narrow limits quite charming work was sometimes
done and many samplers survive, framed, in our homes today.

The Twentieth Century

With the exception of white work and quilting—
and by the end of the century these too had almost died out—the
late 19th century and early 20th century have left us little
embroidery of which to be proud.

Various people, aware of the need for reform, had made sporadic
efforts to improve the quality of needlework. William Morris
(1834–96) as a young man, appalled by the design of everything
machine-made around him, decided to devote his life to re-estab-
lishing honest workmanship in all crafts. With a group of friends
he determined to achieve sound standards of design and began as
early as 1857 to experiment with embroidery in vegetable dyed
yarns on home-spun fabric. Unable to find suitably coloured wools

for his work, he sent them to be dyed in France, then learned the dyer's craft himself. His embroideries, which now look too much like paintings, had little influence on his own generation, but stimulated the arts and crafts movement in Sweden. William Morris could not, however, stem the flow, which continued in the first quarter of the 20th century, of an amazing number of fussy knicknacks appearing in equally fussy and diverse styles, all revived from past eras.

We must remember with respect Flora Klickmann, an embroideress who, though writing in the flowery idiom of her time in the women's magazines she edited, often showed good sense and a sincere love of her craft. In one of her small books twenty different kinds of embroidery and embroidered laces, with photographs of partly worked specimens, are mentioned, and to her must be given some of the credit for keeping alive an interest in embroidery technique, however debased the design.

A far greater feeling for embroidery was evident in the work of Mrs. A. H. Christie, who fully appreciated the greatness of our historical tradition and, through her practical approach and extensive academic study, prepared the way for a re-awakening of interest in design, accompanied by a desire to experiment with fabrics and embroidery techniques, which began about 1925. One of the leaders in the fresh approach was Rebecca Crompton, a versatile designer who worked fast and appeared to be capable of translating all her ideas into stitchery. Much of her embroidery was in appliqué, using a wide assortment of textures and tones, usually in

79 *"The Yellow Dog" by Rebecca Crompton, worked in mallard floss and sequins on a white velvet ground*

delicate colour schemes, constructed with fairly large stitches (79). She did, however, also experiment with detailed work, including the spiral use of chain and split stitch and the effect of light upon it based on the method used in Opus Anglicanum. A travelling exhibition of her work in the early 1930's made a telling impact upon a number of potential designers.

If Mrs. Crompton's style now appears rather self-conscious the same comment can be made about embroidery only ten years old, so rapid are present day changes in outlook. Since her time embroidery has passed through several phases; some framed pictorial work has been trivial, not developing beyond sketch book scribbles which have masqueraded as spontaneity, too often unsupported by sound technique. Nowadays much very good work is done. Designers exploring the use of colour and texture have a far more lively approach to subject matter than hitherto. Fortunately their work is becoming known to a much wider public.

Interest has been fostered by Art Colleges and Colleges of Further Education; by the Royal School of Needlework, which has a deserved reputation for meticulous technique; and by the Townswomen's Guild and the Women's Institute. Immediately after the 1939–45 War, the Needlework Development Scheme did more than any other body to promote the spread of ideas through its publications and travelling collections which contained work, both historical and modern, from many countries. Its contribution to the teaching of embroidery cannot be overestimated.

Throughout this whole period the Embroiderers' Guild has gained strength, expanded its excellent library and travelling collections and now offers an increasingly rich variety of short courses on all aspects of the craft. It owns a valuable collection of English and foreign embroidery. The Guild actively encourages the craft through its frequent exhibitions.

Subject matter and execution are no longer bound by convention, with strange results. Fashion can tempt designers to revert to earlier styles or, with an unlimited range of materials at their disposal, they can be so intent upon finding an unusual viewpoint that some work contains more scrap iron than stitchery. It has been questioned whether geometric work without stitchery, involving the play of light on a subtle arrangement of fabrics, can be called embroidery. Experiments in this field have been made by Jennifer Gray, with fascinating results which are certainly an aspect of textile design. Other contemporary embroiderers work with macramé, crochet and knitting in conjunction with stitchery. We are now more deeply concerned than ever before with the problems of colour and texture and prepared to exploit all manner of threads to achieve an effect. Current design trends are reflected in an increased use of suede and leather and in semi-transparent

80 *Mitre designed in 1938 for Guildford Cathedral*

curtain gauzes obtainable in different weights which, though intended for hangings and room-dividers, lend themselves to large scale pulled fabric work, needle-weaving and other devices.

Many of these curtain gauzes come from Scandinavian countries which, in the mid-20th century, influenced English embroidery design. Their combination of sound technique with an innate sense of colour and a refreshing simplification of form now appears to have been assimilated and the origin already forgotten.

ECCLESIASTICAL EMBROIDERY

Although much embroidery is no longer bound by convention there are instances where the very nature of the work required imposes a necessary discipline. Church embroidery design received a fresh impetus after the last World War. Coventry Cathedral, begun in 1955, needed full ecclesiastical regalia, altar cloths and fair linen, lectern falls and kneelers. Other churches, rebuilt after wartime destruction, such as St. Clement Dane's, among countless others, and those in "new towns", had similar if more modest requirements, and many gave encouragement to potential embroiderers with requests for assistance in carrying out designs.

During the first half of the 20th century much church embroidery had been basically weak in design, and particularly unfortunate in the treatment of the human figure, which was either sentimental or mannered. Compared with Opus Anglicanum it was stiff and not drawn with the compulsion that springs from intensity of vision and religious fervour. Too many banners give the impression that the mere use of brocade, gold thread, cord and fringe translate any design into a piece of ecclesiastical embroidery, and there are to be found regrettable examples with painted heads, hands and feet. Illegible lettering is another grave fault.

Immediately after the war a small group of trained designers corrected this unhappy state of affairs. Kathleen Whyte, Barbara Dawson, and Beryl Dean are foremost amongst those specialising in ecclesiastical embroidery. Pat Russell has shown how stimulating lettering can be whether used with an academic attitude towards form and spacing or with an approach even more difficult to handle, in which legibility becomes subordinate to pattern. Precedent for a craftsman's use of lettering as a border pattern can be seen in late mediaeval brasses where the engraved figure is often contained within a "black letter" inscription which, though almost illegible, makes a good strong band of vertical lines.

Already many handsome designs in magnificent colour are to be found and there is plenty of evidence that by the end of the century ecclesiastical embroidery will have emerged completely from the doldrums of 100 years ago.

Pictures

The embroidered picture conceived as a separate entity first appeared in the 17th century, when it became possible to distinguish between pictorial hangings and the picture designed for no other purpose than to be framed. Subjects were taken from the Old Testament, the Apocrypha and classical mythology, or were allegorical, or pastoral in theme.

A picture of 1620 shows Jesse peacefully resting on his elbow, watching with some interest a woman and parrot, quite unperturbed by the tree above him, full of his descendants each overflowing a floral nest. There is the usual complete disregard for scale; the rose, tulip, carnation and lily are drawn larger than the human beings. Every space is filled with leaf, flower or bud, building or domestic scene. The background is covered with long and short stitch in silk and a variety of patterned fillings.

Another picture of the Queen of Sheba before King Solomon, worked 1625–50, is in tent stitch. The landscape is English, with a Jacobean mansion in the background, a barn, pear tree, pansies, an iris, pinks, a rose, butterflies, birds, a duck on a pond, and in the midst of all these, the king on a throne in a tent, his courtier, and the queen with an attendant lady. Often in such pictures the reigning monarch is faithfully portrayed. Parham, in Sussex, has a fine collection of embroidered pictures belonging to this period.

Edmund Harrison, a professional embroiderer and member of the London Broderers' company, worked in the mid-17th century. His "Adoration of the Shepherds" (V. & A.) (3′ 7″ × 2′ 4½″; signed and dated 1637), is in an entirely different style from the work of his contemporaries, being strongly influenced by late Flemish painting, and embroidered in a technique used on the Continent more often than in England, that is, shaded couching in coloured silk over parallel lines of gold thread. Long and short, brick, split and satin stitches are also used. Each figure is worked separately then applied. Such a method had freed itself from any need to imitate the texture of tapestry weaving, only to acquire a new and more dangerous limitation, that of imitating the painted picture.

At this time also embroidered portraits, influenced by miniatures, came into fashion. Several similar portraits of Charles I, in the manner of Van Dyck, show technical virtuosity; they are worked upon satin in coloured floss silk, chiefly in split stitch slightly padded in a masterly simulation of lace on the wide collar, though this may indicate a later date. Each is mounted in a metal setting as for a miniature.

Not all were so skilful and successful as for instance a portrait of a lady of the reign of Charles I, worked on satin, using long and short and chain stitch, French knots and velvet stitch. A pastoral scene occupies the background space within the raised wreath which surrounds the portrait. The wreath is elaborate, made from strips of parchment bound with silk thread, alternating with loops of gimp. Pictures in the 17th century were indeed diverse in style, from refined black silk imitations of engravings to curious stump work; and apart from this latter fall from grace, techniques were similar throughout the 18th century, with remarkably little change in subject matter. Until 1720 the lions and leopards of Oriental influence persist, but seldom occur later. Royal portraits also belong to the early years of the century. Pastoral scenes increased in number, as did imitations of engravings, and from about 1775 to these were added copies of pictures by Morland, Gainsborough and Fragonard. Panels could be bought ready prepared upon silk with the sky, hands and faces painted in water-colour to be left exposed when the embroidery in long stitches in coloured silk and wool was completed.

Mary Linwood (1755–1845) acquired great skill and consequent fame for her copies of paintings. She worked on a specially woven woollen cloth called tammy, and had wools dyed for her. Her copies of engravings on sarsenet, in brown or black silk found many imitators.

Some pictures were worked in a wider range of stitches, stem, long and short, braid, satin, seeding, French knots, bullions, in an attempt to reproduce texture—a lamb might be worked all over in knot stitch; while about 1780 chenille, used for fur and trees, was regarded as a labour-saving device.

Towards the end of the century occurs the forerunner of 20th-century "fabric collage", oil-paintings copied in tailors' cuttings, in many small pieces laid one upon the other making an uneven surface. The pictorial achievements of the 19th century in Berlin woolwork have been mentioned in an earlier chapter.

Pictorial machine embroidery worked on commercial machines by trained designers is a very recent development (from 1938), yet within a short time it became sufficiently established to be considered in its own right. Access to specialised machines is normally through an Art College but there are now several domestic sewing machines capable of producing a variety of patterns. Machine embroidery can be used alone or with hand embroidery, on transparent materials, gauzes, and on heavier fabrics with equal success (81).

81 *Part of a panel by Moyra Somerville in machine embroidery with some applied net*

Pictorial embroiderers of the second half of the 20th century have shown great versatility in choice of materials. A new development calling for skilled presentation makes use of frail webs of stitchery on fabrics placed at different levels, one or more inches apart, those above having holes cut in them to expose work beneath. Other experimenters build outwards with raised blocks and cylinders covered with fabric and/or embroidery. Some designs intended for wall decoration appear to be influenced by geometric, problem-solving exercises, while other work seems to arise directly from unexpected objects which have been applied, an alliance between collage and stitchery. Many designers still cling fairly closely to natural form and we are all, through the television media, encouraged to grow more perceptive to secrets revealed by photography; highly magnified microscopic life and the colour and pattern of marine creatures, now seen for the first time by virtue of underwater cameras. This is certainly an age of experiment.

Embroidered Book Bindings

After the invention of printing the interest previously shown in illumination of the hand-written page diminished and

more attention was given to the book binding itself. Private
libraries were gradually created and books, being valuable, were
bound in tooled leather. Leather bindings developed more elaborately on the Continent than in England, where instead, embroidered
bindings predominated. About 250 years elapsed between the
earliest embroidered book binding, the Felbrigge Psalter, and the
last, believed to have been made at the end of the 17th century;
bindings were the height of fashion for about a hundred years,
from mid 16th to mid 17th century, and the fashion arose of
covering any book of particular importance, especially if it were a
New Year gift, with an embroidered binding, sometimes so rich
that an embroidered protective covering, a development of the
mediaeval forel, was also made.

Since there are comparatively few Continental embroidered
book bindings this may be regarded as a peculiarly English
fashion.

Embroidered bookcovers were made for bibles, prayer books,
devotional books such as *Daily Exercise of a Christian*, 1623, with
bees on the spine symbolising industry, books of psalms and the
New Testament. These varied greatly in size, from the very thin
book $2'' \times 3''$ with $\frac{3}{4}''$ spine and in the double book,[1] or dos à dos,
$2'' \times 4''$ with $2''$ spine, to a probable maximum of $17'' \times 12''$. Most
were much smaller, about $3'' \times 6''$.

There are distinct styles according to whether the ground is
velvet, satin, fine canvas or linen covered with metal thread.

In all styles the book is given a spine divided into compartments,
each with a small motif which may be repeated several times.
There are exceptions to every rule, so a very few books with
undivided spines do exist.

Both back and front of the book are invariably the same.

DESIGNS UPON VELVET

Designs on red, purple or fawn velvet usually include an interlacing
arabesque border surrounding a central motif of initials, a coat of
arms denoting ownership or a religious scene.

The border is worked in metal thread, silver and silver-gilt, in
more than one thickness, often very much raised and padded. It is

---

[1] A double book consists of two distinct volumes bound together and read from
opposite ends. One may be the Book of Common Prayer and the other the Psalms.

82 *Binding for a Bible, 1583, worked in gold, silver and coloured silks with a few seed pearls in the border, on crimson velvet; 16⅝" × 11⅝", spine about 4¼" thick.* 83 *Binding, first half 17th century, 13" × 9" worked in gold and silver thread on red velvet, enclosing a prayer book*

doubtful whether this was done consciously to protect the velvet. Seed pearls add a lighter tone and are usually grouped closely together for that purpose.

The central motif may be in the same style or, in small books, worked in silk with long and short stitch; examples of this style dated 1540, 1543 and 1544 may be seen in the British Museum. The two books illustrated are of slightly later date. The Bible from the Bodleian Library is $16\frac{5}{8}'' \times 11\frac{5}{8}''$ with a spine of about 4″. Printed in 1583 it was offered to Queen Elizabeth I in 1584 by the

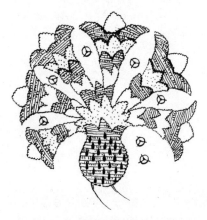

84 *Loose linen cover for a book, $16\frac{1}{2}'' \times 9\frac{1}{4}''$, about 1640, with scrolling floral design embroidered in silk in red, pink, blue, pale blue, green, yellow-green, yellows and orangey (madder) red, chiefly in detached buttonhole, each petal standing separately; darning, bullion knots and spangles and some gold thread are also used*

printer as a New Year gift, and according to the gift roll, "Venice" gold was used(82). With silver thread, coloured silks and a few seed pearls on crimson velvet, an exceedingly handsome book was made. The second illustration is one of a pair in a private collection; these, though not so large, a Bible, $14'' \times 9''$ and a prayer book, $13'' \times 9''$ are extremely impressive(83). They were worked in a variety of gold and silver threads upon red velvet during the first half of the 17th century.

DESIGNS ON LINEN OR FINE CANVAS

Bindings worked on linen or fine canvas are covered entirely with very small tent stitch worked in silk. In a cover made in 1581 the tent stitch is worked in one direction for the background and the opposite way for a formal floral design outlined, for further emphasis, with silver-gilt thread. This is a restrained piece of work in dull yellows with a touch of blue-green upon a fawn ground. Plaited stitch is worked in silver round the edge of the book. Tent stitch designs are more often pictorial, as in one dated 1612, where Jacob and the Angel disport themselves in an English country setting.

SILK AND SATIN BINDINGS

Satin bindings are often of red or a pale pink sometimes faded to a soft fawn. They are embroidered in silk in long and short stitch and long satin stitch, laid-work and couching, with a wealth of spangles. Metal thread is used lavishly, in silver and silver-gilt, in plate, purl, passing and bullion, and coloured blue and pink, with surprisingly pleasant results. The designs on satin are varied and follow fairly closely the trends of the same date. A binding of 1605, upon a pale pink satin ground, has a central medallion surrounded by flowers and insects. Another, of 1571, of red satin, $3'' \times 5\frac{1}{2}''$, has an arabesque border incorporating gold fabric outlined with silver-gilt and bullions. The central medallion is a "cameo", one centimetre diameter, of a woman's head, Italian style, in silk stitchery. One of the later silk bindings, a New Testament of 1640, is almost stump work, and within the small space of $2'' \times 4''$ are crowded several insects and one flower worked in tent stitch on canvas afterwards applied, while needlepoint is used for a goldfinch on a columbine, a daffodil and a butterfly. The butterfly's lower wings and the columbine's lower petals are worked direct upon the fabric, but the upper wings and other flower petals are worked separately to stand away from the background. On this particular book there is room for only a very few spangles. The spine is clumsy with a highly embossed lily, pansy, and rose in separate compartments, worked in silver thread and silk buttonhole stitch. This tiny, elaborate book with its silver plaited edge, must have been a great joy to its recipient.

BINDINGS MAINLY IN METAL THREAD

One of the earliest in this style is traditionally said to have been worked by Princess Elizabeth, about 1544, as a New Year gift for Queen Katherine Parr. This uninspired piece of work may well have been the dutiful gift of an eleven-year-old step-daughter. It is embroidered in chain stitch in gold and silver on blue corded silk, and is so well done that it looks like fabric. Owned by the Bodleian

Library, this book with its inscription and dedication in Elizabeth's hand, is of far greater historical than artistic interest.

Though less beautiful than the satin and velvet bindings, those which are almost wholly covered with metal thread are extremely interesting on close examination. They are heavily embossed and where the thread has worn away the method of padding with couching and satin stitch can be seen. Colour variation is attained by using silver and the warmer toned silver-gilt and by couching the metal with different coloured silks, as in a Bible of 1626 which has a smooth silver thread couched in blue silk to form a diamond

85   *Detail from Bible, 1638 (B. Mus.).
Angel's head in various types of metal thread.
The face is padded beneath laid-work and the
long feathers are of plate, i.e. thin flat strips
of metal*

diaper pattern and twisted silver thread couched with yellow in a brick pattern. Metal is also couched with metal. The silver purl is itself often tinted blue, pink or red and is sewn down in various ways to give different textures, frequently tightly looped and curled for flower petals. Spangles fill every available space. In the illustration (85) the angel's wings are of long metal strips known as plate, only lightly attached, to give a convincing appearance of feathers; that they have endured for so long points to very careful ownership of a heavy, rather clumsily designed, but sturdy book.

The British Museum has a very fine collection of embroidered book bindings. Others may be seen at the Bodleian Library, the British and Foreign Bible Society, the Victoria and Albert Museum, at Little Gidding, in many private collections both here and in U.S.A.—sufficient proof of their great popularity.

Bibliography

A. General

Alexander, E. *Fabric Pictures* (Mills and Boon, 1959)
Alford, Lady M. *Needlework as Art* (Sampson Low, 1896)
Ashton, A. L. B. *Samplers* (Medici, 1924)

Benson, D. *Your Machine Embroidery* (Sylvan Press, 1952)

Childs & Colles *Christian Symbols: Ancient and Modern* (Bell, 1971)
Christie, A. G. I. *English Mediaeval Embroidery* (O.U.P., 1938)
Christie, Mrs. A. *Embroidery and Tapestry Weaving* (Pitman, 1906)
Colby, Averil *Patchwork* (Batsford, 1959)
Colby, Averil *Samplers* (Batsford, 1964)
Crompton, Rebecca *Modern Design in Embroidery* (Batsford, 1936)

Davenport, C. *English Embroidered Bookbindings* (Kegan Paul, 1899)
Dawson, B. *Metal Thread Embroidery* (Batsford, 1968)
Dean, Beryl *Ecclesiastical Embroidery* (Batsford, 1960)
Digby, G. W. *Elizabethan Embroidery* (Faber, 1963)

Fitzwilliam, Lady Ada *Jacobean Embroidery* (Kegan Paul, 1912)

Howard, Constance *Designer for Embroidery from Traditional English Sources* (Batsford, 1956)
Huish, Marcus B. *Samplers and Tapestry Embroideries* (Longman, 1913)

Jourdain, Margaret *English Secular Embroidery* (Kegan Paul, 1910)

Kendrick, A. F. *English Embroidery* (Batsford, 1910)
Kendrick, A. F. *A Book of Old Embroidery* (Studio, 1921)
Kendrick, A. F. *English Needlework* (Black, 1933)
Kendrick, A. F. *English Decorative Fabrics of Sixteenth to Eighteenth Centuries* (Black, 1934)

Maclagan, E. *Bayeux Tapestry* (King Penguin, 1943)
Morris, B. *Victorian Embroidery* (Barrie & Jenkins, 1962)

Russell, P. *Lettering for Embroidery* (Batsford, 1971)

Seligman & Hughes *Domestic Needlework* (Country Life, 1926)
Stenton, Sir Frank *Bayeux Tapestry* (Phaidon, 1957)
Symonds & Preece *Needlework through the Ages* (Hodder, 1928)
Swain, M. *The Flowerers* (on Ayrshire work) (Chambers, 1955)

Tattersall, C. E. *A History of British Carpets* (F. Lewis, 1934)

Wace, A. J. B. *Mediterranean and Near Eastern Embroideries* (Halton, 1935)

B. Publications of Victoria and Albert Museum
Irwin, J. *Indian Embroidery* (H.M.S.O., 1951)

Maclagan, E. R. D. *Catalogue of English Ecclesiastical Embroidery from the Thirteenth to the Sixteenth Century* (H.M.S.O., 1916)
Morris, B. *History of English Embroidery* (H.M.S.O., 1928)
Nevinson, J. *Catalogue of English Domestic Embroidery of the Sixteenth and Seventeenth Centuries* (H.M.S.O., 1938)

Chair Seats and Backs (H.M.S.O., 1929)
Elizabethan Embroidery (H.M.S.O., 1953)
Fifty Masterpieces of Textiles (H.M.S.O., 1957)
Flowers in English Embroidery (H.M.S.O., 1947)
Samplers (H.M.S.O., 1947)

C. Costume
Bradfield, N. *Costume in Detail 1730–1930* (Harrap, 1968)
Bradfield, N. *Historical Costumes of England 1066–1968* (Harrap, 1970)
Brooke, I. *Dress and Undress: the Restoration and Eighteenth Century* (Methuen, 1958)

Cunnington, C. Willet *Handbook of English Mediaeval Costume* (Faber, 1952)
Cunnington, C. Willet *Handbooks of English Costume*, 4 vols. (Faber, 1967-1972)
Cunnington, C. Willet *The Perfect Lady* (Parrish, 1948)
Cunnington, C. Willet *History of Underclothes* (Michael Joseph, 1951)
Davenport *Book of Costume*, 2 vols (Crown, 1948)
Hansen, H. *Costume Cavalcade* (Methuen, 1956)
Houston, M. *Mediaeval Costume in England and France* (Black, 1939)
Kohler, C. von Sichart, E. *A History of Costume* (Harrap, 1928)
Laver, James *Costume* (Batsford, 1956)
Laver, James *Early Tudor* (Costume of the Western World Series) (Harrap, 1951)
Redfern *Royal and Historic Gloves and Shoes* (Methuen, 1904)
Yarwood, Doreen *English Costume* (Batsford, 1958)

D. Reference Books
Edwards & Ramsey *Concise Encyclopaedia of Antiques*, 2 vols (Connoisseur, 1954–5)
Gass, I. *A Glance at Heraldry* (Harrap, 1959)
Giles, G. Scott *Boutell's Heraldry* (Warne, 1950)
Harrison, David *Tudor England*, vols. I and II (Cassell, 1954)
Mairet, E. *Vegetable Dyes* (Faber, 1952)
Nicholl, A. *The Elizabethans* (C.U.P., 1956)
Pearson, L. E. *The Elizabethans at Home* (Stanford University Press, 1957)
Rice, D. Talbot *English Art 871–1100* (O.U.P., 1952)
Trevelyan, G. M. *Illustrated English Social History*, 4 vols. (Longman 1949–1952)
Wagner, A. *Heraldry in England* (Penguin, 1946)
Yarwood, Doreen *The English Home* (Batsford, 1959)
Connoisseur Period Guides
Encyclopaedia Britannica: Textiles
People, Places and Things (Waverley Press)

Index

The numbers in **bold** type denote the figure numbers of the illustrations

133